FLORENCE

FIESOLE · PRATO · PISTOIA
SAN GIMIGNANO · VOLTERRA · SIENA

Authors:
Ulrike Bleek,
Christiane Büld-Campetti,
Dr. Stephan Bleek,
Kirsten Faber

An Up-to-date travel guide
with 55 color photos
and 10 maps

NELLES

Dear Reader: Being up-to-date is the main goal of the Nelles series. Our correspondents help keep us abreast of the latest developments in the travel scene, while our cartographers see to it that maps are also kept completely current. However, as the travel world is constantly changing, we cannot guarantee that all the information contained in our books is always valid. Should you come across a discrepancy, please contact us at: Nelles Verlag, Schleissheimer Str. 371 b, 80935 Munich, Germany, tel. (089) 3571940, fax. (089) 35719430, e-mail: Nelles.Verlag@t-online.de

Note: Distances and measurements, including temperatures, used in this guide are metric. For conversion information, please see the *Guidelines* section of this book.

LEGEND

★★ ★★	Main Attraction *(on map) (in text)*	**Volterra** *(Town)* **S. Galgano** *(Sight)*	Places Highlighted in Yellow Appear in Text	National Border
★ ★	Worth Seeing *(on map) (in text*	✈ ✈	Int'l, Nat'l Airport	Tollway
❽	Orientation Number in Text and on Map	**Mte. Amiata** 1738	Mountain (altitude in meters)	Expressway Principal Highway
■	Public or Significant Building	\ 13 /	Distance in Kilometers	Main Road Secondary Road
■	Hotel	☀	Beach	Ferry
■	Market	🌳	National Park	P Parking
✝ ⛪	Church	🅸	Tourist Information	SSS Luxury Hotel Category
⛫	Castle	∴	Ancient site	SS Moderate Hotel Category S Budget Hotel Category
		†	Cemetery	*(for price information see "Accomodation" in Guidelines section)*

FLORENCE – Fiesole, Prato, Pistoia, San Gimignano, Volterra, Siena
© Nelles Verlag GmbH, 80935 München
  All rights reserved

First Edition 2000
ISBN 3-88618-267-3 (Nelles Travel Pack)
ISBN 3-88618-773-X (Nelles Pocket)
Printed in Slovenia

Publisher:	Günter Nelles	**Printing:**	Gorenjski Tisk
Managing Editor:	Berthold Schwarz	**Lithos:**	Priegnitz, Munich
Editor:	Chase Stewart	**Cartography:**	Nelles Verlag GmbH
Photo Editor:	K. Bärmann-Thümmel		Munich

LIST OF MAPS

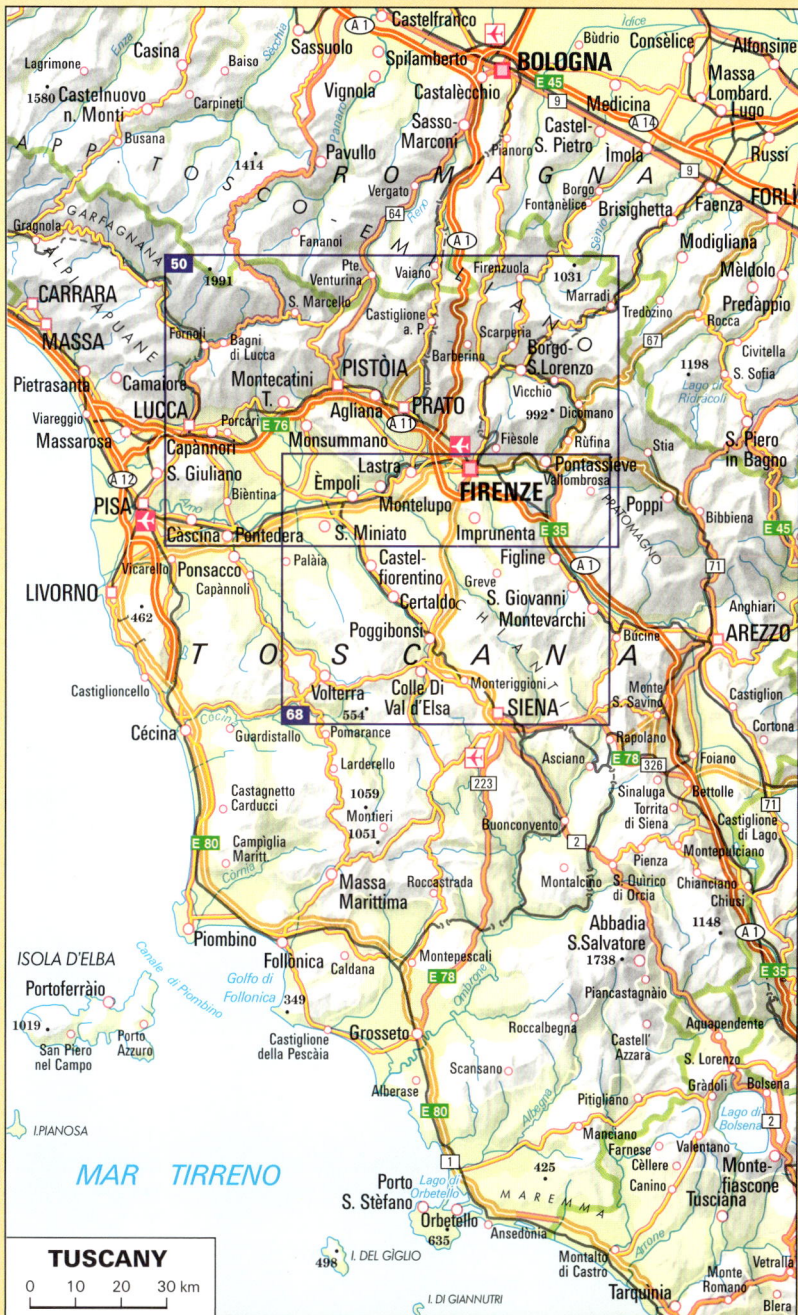

TUSCANY

0 10 20 30 km

Early History and Antiquity

2nd millennium B.C. In the Bronze Age, Indo-Germanic peoples migrate from the north to the region that is present-day Tuscany. Among them are the Italic tribes, from whose language group the Romans descended.

Circa 1000 B.C. At the beginning of the Iron Age, the Illyrians migrate to this region from Asia Minor.

8th-3rd centuries B.C. The Etruscans settle in an area which extends far beyond the boundaries of present-day Tuscany, reaching as far south as the area around Naples. The precise origin of the Etruscans, who were highly developed both technically and artistically, remains unknown. The Romans later named them Tusci, from which Tuscan and later Toscana (Tuscany) evolved. The Greek culture makes headway into northern Italy through busy trading relationships.

753 B.C. The legendary founding of Rome precipitates the decline of the powerful Etruscans.

474 B.C. The Etruscans suffer a devastating defeat at the hands of the Syracusan fleet in the Battle of Cumae.

396 B.C. The Romans conquer Veii, 30 kilometers north of Rome. It is the most important southern city-state of the Etruscans.

295 B.C. In the Battle of Sentium (Sassoferrato, near Fabriano), Rome defeats the Etruscans once and for all.

217 B.C. Hannibal defeats the Romans at Lake Trasimene. In the course of further battles with Rome, however, the Carthiginian ruler fails to break the power of the Romans.

A.D. 59 Under Caesar, the veteran's colony of *Florentia* – later Florence – is founded on an important trade route, the *Via Cassia*.

Middle Ages

408 The Goths conquer Italy.

476-553 The Ostrogoths under Odoacer and Theodoric the Great rule Italy.

568-774 The Lombards found the Duchy of Tuscian.

774 Charlemagne, who makes three trips to Florence, conquers the Lombard empire and declares Tuscian a Frankish margravate.

Circa 1000 Margave Hugo moves his residence to Florence. The red and white of his coat-of-arms are now the city's colors.

1046-1115 Under the rule of Margravine Matilda, Tuscian reaches its political zenith. During the time of the investiture controversy, in which the popes fight against the emperor, the cities of Tuscian enter into alliances with conflicting parties. Matilda, however, supports Pope Gregory VII, and it is in her castle on the northern slopes of the Apennines that Henry IV makes his famous journey to Canossa, which is forced on him by Rome, to do penance on his knees before the Pope in order to have his sentence of excommunication lifted.

Emperor Henry IV with Margravine Matilda before his journey to Canossa (contemporary book illumination).

1115 After the death of Margravine Matilda, all her Tuscan possessions go to the Church. Cities such as Florence and Siena claim increasing independence and develop into oligarchical city-states.

13th century All the cities of northern Italy are involved in a feud between the Ghibellines, who support the emperor, and the Guelphs, who support the Pope. This feud erupts into street battles (compare the story of *Romeo and Juliet*).

13th-14th centuries In spite of civil-war-like conditions, trade thrives. Poets such as Dante Alighieri (1265-1321), Francesco Petrarca (1304-74) and Giovanni Boccaccio (1313-75) influence literature, while artists such as Giotto, Gaddi and the Pisanos lead the fine arts of the time into the Renaissance. Florence claims hegemony over Tuscany. By conquest or purchase, the cities of Fiesole, Pistoia, Prato, San Gimignano and Volterra yield to Florentine rule. Siena does not come under the yoke of Florence until 1559.

Duke Cosimo I – scion of the mighty Medici banking family – enriched Florence with the Uffizi (painting by J. Caruca).

15th century Thanks to artists such as Brunelleschi, Massaccio, Masolino and Donatello, art sees a renaissance of ancient forms. Masterpieces such as the dome of the Cathedral of Florence (Brunelleschi) and the doors of the Baptistery (Ghiberti) are created. In the age of humanism, power in Florence falls into the hands of the Medici family, who prove themselves to be outstanding patrons of the arts.

1488 Michelangelo Buonarotti joins the workshop of Domenico Ghirlandaio in Florence, and is soon accepted into the court school of the Medicis.

1497 The Medici family is driven out of Florence. The Dominican monk Girolamo Savonarola (1452-98) attempts political renewal on the basis of republican principles. He fails and is burned at the stake.

1501-1505 Michelangelo returns to Florence. His famous *David* and the so-called *Madonna Pitti* are created during this period.

1512 Return of the Medicis to Florence.

1531 Emperor Charles V makes Alessandro de' Medici, supposedly an illegitimate son of Pope Clement VII, Duke of Florence. After his assassination in 1537, Cosimo de' Medici becomes Duke of Florence and reigns for 37 years.

1570 Cosimo conquers Siena and is appointed Grand Duke of Tuscany by Pope Pius V.

1574-1737 After the death of Cosimo, the Medicis continue to rule Tuscany as grand dukes, but their power begins to decline.

1633 Galileo Galilei, a scientist in the service of the Grand Duke, is persecuted by the Inquisition and is forced to renounce his teaching of a heliocentric planetary system.

1743 After the end of the Medici Dynasty, Tuscany is handed over to the House of Habsburg.

1799-1815 Napoleon conquers Italy. Tuscany is ruled by his sister Elisa

1815 The Congress of Vienna rules that Tuscany be returned to the House of Habsburg-Lorraine.

1848-59 The first War of Independence in 1848 expels the Habsburgs, but only briefly. Not until the referendum of 1859 can Tuscany be joined to the Kingdom of Piedmont.

1865-71 After Victor Emmanuel II of Piedmont is proclaimed King of Italy in 1861, he at first establishes Florence as his capital city.

1946 After the end of fascism, the Republic of Italy is declared on June 2.

1966 The metropolis on the Arno is devastated by the worst floods in the city's history.

1993 A bomb attack is carried out on the Galleria degli Uffizi, home of the most-visited art collection in Italy and one of the world's largest art museums. Restoration of the damage and a planned extension are not expected to be completed before the end of the year 2000.

AROUND FLORENCE

FLORENCE
AROUND FLORENCE / FIESOLE
MUGELLO / SIEVETAL
PRATO / PISTOIA
ARNO VALLEY / MONTALBANO

**FLORENCE
The Blossoming City**

When the French writer Stendhal visited Florence on his journey to Italy some two hundred years ago, he was so overwhelmed by the beauty of the city that he genuinely fell ill. To this day, there are still repeated instances of tourists having to be hospitalized because they come down with "Stendhal syndrome": so great is the abundance of cultural monuments which people think they absolutely must see before they leave that many are driven into a state of hysteria bordering on nervous breakdown. Only Italians appear to be immune to this phenomenon; at least this is the conclusion that was reached by a scientific study.

It's simply impossible to "see" or truly get to know ****Florence ❶** in a matter of only a few days; indeed, weeks if not months would be required in order to accomplish this task. The city is so inexhaustibly rich in sights – and not just cultural ones – that it is definitely a better idea to take your time and limit yourself to those works of art which come closest to your own personal tastes and interests.

Preceding pages: View of Florence from the Piazzale Michelangelo. Left: Graceful, open-minded and stylish – truly Florentine

In addition, you should let the flavor of the city and its life work on you, and, last but not least, reserve some time for shopping, as in this last respect Florence is also tempting in the extreme.

In the restricted space at our disposal here, it will, of course, be impossible to provide exhaustive information about Florence. There are plenty of detailed studies available for those who want to immerse themselves in the history, art and culture of the city, and a visit to a bookstore or library would serve the traveler well. We will limit ourselves to an overview of the most important works of art and buildings in the city.

The City's Early History

Back in the time of the Etruscans, there was already a settlement on the banks of the Arno, and it was here that the Romans established a veterans' colony for former legionnaires in 59 B.C.; in other words, at the time of Caesar. The colony was named *Colonia Florentia*, the "blossoming colony": perhaps because the fertile Arno Valley has such an abundance of flowers. There are a number of theories about the true origins of the name, but none of them is really convincing.

Because of its exposed location on the river in the midst of the hilly Tuscan land-

could be transported down to the Mediterranean; and the traders from the East who started settling here brought with them Christianity, which began its steady progress after A.D. 300. The 4th century saw the construction of the first two Christian churches: San Lorenzo, which at that time was located outside the city walls, and Santa Felicità, on the opposite bank of the Arno. As early as the year 313, the first bishop was appointed under Emperor Constantine.

Under the Romans, marble palaces and temples dominated the cityscape, while an aqueduct brought water down from Monte Morelli to supply the city's residents with drinking water and fill the public baths. A huge amphitheater was built during the 2nd century A.D.; you can still detect its outlines in the curving façades of the houses on the Via de' Bentaccordi and the Via Torta.

scape, the settlement was hardly suitable as a military base, so we can assume that right from the start it had primarily an agricultural function. Its defense was secured by the hilltop town of Fiesole, just a few miles away, an old stronghold of the Etruscans, in whose shadow the *Colonia Florentia* had a fairly insignificant existence for quite some time.

The earliest ground plan of the city on the right bank of the Arno formed an almost perfect rectangle, the outlines of which still largely correspond to the heart of the Old Town today. Because of its favorable location on the *Via Cassia*, which ran from Rome through Florence and went on to Lucca, and because of the connecting roads to the other most important cities of what was then the province of Etruria, Florence rapidly developed into an important trade center in the first two hundred years after its foundation. A harbor on the Arno River meant that goods

Florence in the Middle Ages

This first flowering, which may have seen the city's population swell to almost 10,000, came to an end in the confusion of the great barbarian migrations. Florence was attacked and devastated by the Ostrogoths, the Byzantines and the Lombards in turn. After the fall of the Roman Empire, traders and merchants stayed away, as the new power constellation meant that trade routes had shifted west and east of the Arno Valley. When the Western Roman Empire fell in the 5th century, the inhabited part of Florence had shrunk to a small area around the old Roman forum, which lives on today, in shape and size, in the form of the current Piazza della Repubblica.

The only event of importance for the art historian during this period was the first phase of construction of the Santa Reparata, the church which preceded the Cathedral. Work may well also have started on a forerunner of the present Baptistery.

Above: Cathedral, Campanile and Baptistery in Florence. Right: San Miniato al Monte.

Not until the Franks under Charlemagne conquered large parts of Italy and proclaimed Tuscany a margravate did the economy begin to take off again. In 854, Lothar I combined the two duchies of Florence and Fiesole and established Florence as the seat of government, which brought with it numerous privileges for the city. Prosperity increased; Florence's population rose to 20,000; and soon the city had spread to take over the left bank of the Arno, as well. The churches of San Lorenzo and Santa Reparata were expanded, and with the construction of the monastery and the basilica of San Miniato, as well as the Baptistery, we have the first manifestations of the Florentine Romanesque style. In 978, Willa, the widow of the margrave Umberto, founded the *Badia fiorenta* and thereby the first monastery in the city.

The clergy, already endowed with large estates, now began to strive for more and more political power, and ecclesiastical offices were sold off to the highest bidder. A monk named Giovanni Gualberto protested against the increasing immorality of the Church, but found little response from the Florentines. He left the city to live as a hermit in the Vallombrosa forest, where he founded the order of the Vallombrosans.

The 11th century was a period marked by the increasing self-confidence of the middle class. Craftsmen, artisans and merchants were gaining in influence. Their struggle for autonomy was, moreover, supported by the margravine Matilda of Canossa, who to protect the Church from secular intervention took the Pope's side in the struggle between the Pope and the Emperor. After her death in 1115, Florence proclaimed a government of its own, which was officially recognized by the Emperor in 1183.

The Period of Communal Constitution

When the empire temporarily lost its grip on Italy after the death of Henry V (1125), nothing more stood in the way of

FLORENCE

Via Jacopo da Diacceto
Via L. Alamanni
Via Nazionale
Via Guelfa
★Sant'Apollonia ⑬
⑫ ★San Marco
Università
Pza. S. Marco
Via Cavour
Via Battisti
S.S. Annunziata
★San Onofrio ⑱
Via Faenza
Mercato Centrale di San Lorenzo
⑰
Stazione Centrale di S. Maria Novella
Pza. della Stazione
★Galleria dell'Accademia ⑪
Via Ricasoli
Via di Ginori
ℹ
Pza. della Santissima Annunziata ⑭
Ospeda d'Innoce
Via della Scala
Pza. dell'Unità Italiana
⑯
★★San Lorenzo
Pza. S. Lorenzo
⑮ Palazzo Medici-Riccardi
Rotonda di Brunelleschi
Via degli Alfa
★Sta. Maria Novella ⑲
SANTA MARIA
Via Palazzuolo
Pza. S. Maria Novella
Via de Panzani
Via dei Pucci
Via de Martelli
SAN GIOVANNI
Ospedale S. Maria Nuova
Via S. Egidio
Borgo Ognissanti
NOVELLA
Via de Cerretani
★Sta. Maria del Fiore (Duomo) ②
Museo dell'Opera del Duomo
Via d. Agli
★★Battistero ③
S. Giovanni
⑥ Ognissanti
Pza. D'Ognissanti
Ospedale San Giovanni di Dio
Via de Rossi
Via della Spada
Via di Campidoglio
Loggia del Bigallo
Campanile
Campanile
Via dell'Oriuolo
Museo di Antropologia
Lungarno Amerigo Vespucci
Arno
Via d. Vigna Nuova
Pza. Goldini
Via d. Panone
㉓ Palazzo Strozzi
Pza. degli Strozzi
Pza. della Repubblica
Casa di Dante
Via del Corso
Via del Proconsolo
Borgo degli Albizi
Pza. di Cestello
Lungarno Soderini
Ponte Alla Carraia
Lungarno Corsini
㉕ Palazzo Corsini
Pza. S. Trinità ㉒
Santa Trinità
Orsanmichele ④
Via Dante A.
⑧
Via Ghibellina
⑦ Bargello
Teatro Verdi
Via G. Verdi
Pza. del Carmine
Via S. Monaca
Ponte S. Trinità
㉑ Palazzo Davanzati
Porta Rossa
Via
㉔
Lungarno Acciaiuoli
Loggia del Mercato Nuovo
⑳
Pza. della Signoria
⑤ Palazzo Vecchio
Via d. Gondi
Badia
Via San Firenze
S. Firenze
Borgo de Greci
Pza. S. Cro
SANTA CROCE
㉙ Santa Maria del Carmine
Via de Serragli
Via S. Spirito
Borgo S. Jacopo
Santo Spirito
㉗ ★Ponte Vecchio
Loggia dei Lanzi
★★Galleria degli Uffizi ⑥
Via dei Neri
Lung. Archibusieri
San Croce
ℹ
Biblioteca Nazionale ①
Borgo S. Croce
Via de Benci
Pza. ㉘ S. Spirito
SANTO SPIRITO
Via Maggio
Via Guicciardini
Pza. S. Maria Sopr.
Lungarno Gen. Diaz
Arno
Lungarno Torrigiani
Via de Bardi
Ponte Alle Grazie
Lungarno Serristori
Sant' Agostino
Via della Chiesa
Pza. dei Pitti
Pza. S. Felice
㉚ ★Palazzo Pitti
Costa di S. Giorgio
Via di S. Niccolo
Giardano Torrigiani, Porta Romana
Via Romana
Forte di Belvedere
㉜
㉛ ★Giardino di Boboli

FLORENCE

0   250 m   Bobolino

14

Florence's rise to independence. The conquest and destruction of Fiesole marked the start of Florentine domination of the surrounding territories, a domination which continued to expand. Commerce and trade were growing inexorably, and the city spread rapidly. Contacts with Pisa facilitated sea trade with countries in the eastern Mediterranean.

In the 12th century, Florence proclaimed a communal constitution in which the power of government lay with the aristocracy and leading members of the merchant classes. The social pre-eminence of the nobility was expressed in unmistakable terms by the dynastic residential towers which once dominated the city's skyline. During the savage feuds that raged in the 12th century between various aristocratic families, these towers turned into regular fortresses.

Outside the city, too, there were bloody conflicts with the feudal lords, who were gradually subjugated and stripped of their autonomy.

Disputes between the noble families led to a change in the communal constitution. The business of governing was taken over by a *podestà*, a professional politician who regulated public affairs on the basis of newly-developed legal standards.

A typical feature of public life in Florence at that time was the formation of various associations, which then proceeded to develop active, and often bitter, rivalries between one another. This resulted in a state of political instability which, however, proved greatly beneficial to the city's cultural development. Since each party was attempting to outdo the next, they all commissioned new buildings which were intended to demonstrate the status and greatness of the group in question. This was the heyday of the Romanesque style in Florence; a style characterized by clear lines, balanced proportions, a restrained use of color and materials (mainly white and green marble), and geometric patterns.

Another major influence on the city's art and culture was exerted by the monastic orders, which had been settling in Florence since the beginning of the 13th century. The Franciscans built a small church on the site of what was later to be the basilica of Santa Croce; the Dominicans established themselves on the western outskirts of the city, where Santa Maria Novella was built towards the end of the century. Both of these churches functioned as schools which soon came to enjoy an international reputation; Dante, in fact, was a pupil here. The squares in front of the churches were arenas for festive celebrations or the competitions that were so popular with the Florentines.

In addition to these two mendicant orders, numerous other religious communities settled in Florence and built their monasteries there. One rather unusual or-

Above: Representation of the Blacksmiths' Guild on Orsanmichele in Florence. Right: Ponte Santa Trinità over the Arno.

der was the Humiliates, who had immigrated from northern Italy and were later to prove of great economic importance for Florence, turning their hands to the cloth weaving and dyeing trades and maintaining their own workshops.

The Guilds

By far and away the most important of all the associations and organizations which formed in the 13th century were the guilds (*arti*), associations of merchants and craftsmen. Not only did these guilds control trade and commerce, but they also wielded considerable political power. In addition, they put up money for major artistic projects.

The oldest and most influential guild was the Guild of the Calimala, whose trade connections extended from northern Europe to the Near East. Its members were cloth traders, but they were also active as money changers right from the start, and were soon handling not only the banking business of their trade partners

but also of entire aristocratic families. This close affiliation between manufacturing, trade and financial matters was a trademark of Florence's economy and the secret of its tremendous success. The concrete symbol of this ascent to financial power was the *florin*, a gold coin which was first minted in 1252.

The power struggle between the Guelphs, the followers of the Pope, and the Ghibellines, who were loyal to the Emperor, continued to divide the city until the Guelphs finally got the upper hand after the death of Emperor Frederick II in 1250. One of the victims of this feud was Italy's greatest poet, Dante Alighieri, a Ghibelline who was banished from his home town in 1302, and who died in exile in Ravenna 19 years later, a bitter and lonely man.

The prosperity and growing self-confidence of Florence's middle class during the 13th century was expressed in a new need to beautify the city. Numerous squares were enlarged and new streets laid out, which, according to the government's plan, were to be attractive, broad and straight. The Santa Trinità bridge was built at this time. In 1296, work was started on the *Duomo*, or Cathedral, and the Palazzo Vecchio was begun three years later.

The 14th century, by contrast, was characterized by internal and external conflicts, natural catastrophes and economic collapse. In 1333, a huge flood devastated the city; in 1348, more than a third of the population died after an outbreak of the plague; in 1378, the city's poor rebelled in the so-called Uprising of the Ciompi (wool-carders), who stormed the Palazzo Vecchio and forced the election of Salvestro de' Medici as *gonfaloniere* (chief magistrate).

After this "proletarian revolution," the city was governed for a short period by the lower classes, but they soon had to relinquish their power to the great families, who were continuing to become more and more influential, until finally the Medici family took over the reigns of power.

The Medicis

Despite the external difficulties and political instability, the middle class in Florence did still manage, even in this turbulent period, to maintain – and indeed improve – its standard of living, and to continue the beautification of the city.

When the Medicis, a successful family of bankers and merchants, came to power in the city in the year 1434, with Cosimo il Vecchio (the Elder), there began a period of cultural flowering which reached its zenith under Cosimo's grandson Lorenzo the Magnificent, in an era known as the Florentine Renaissance.

Names such as Sandro Botticelli, Domenico Ghirlandaio, Leonardo da Vinci and Michelangelo Buonarroti come to mind when one thinks of this epoch, which was also the acme of Florence's political power in Italy.

What would the stern Savonarola (above) have thought of this modern grafitti artist's work (right)?

Rivalry among other patrician families came to a head with the Pazzi Conspiracy in the Cathedral on April 26, 1475, in the course of which Lorenzo's brother Giuliano was killed. Even though this attempt to overthrow Medici rule failed, Florence ultimately relinquished its leading position in the arts to Rome.

The inflammatory machinations of the puritanical monk Girolamo Savonarola, who condemned the immoral ways of the Renaissance aristocrats, ultimately led to the Medicis' expulsion from Florence. Savonarola prepared a new republican constitution which remained in effect until 1512. But his sermons against the increasing secularization of the Church attracted the wrath of Pope Alexander VI, and he was burned at the stake in 1498 on the Piazza della Signoria.

The Medicis returned to power in 1512, and several members of the family became popes during the course of the century. Wealth, power and education were at this time in the hands of the aristocracy, who built majestic palaces for themselves and commissioned great works of art. Many other Renaissance masterpieces were also commissioned by the guilds, including Brunelleschi's dome atop the Cathedral.

In 1530, Alessandro de' Medici was appointed Grand Duke of Tuscany by Emperor Charles V, and Florence and Tuscany were to remain under the absolutist control of the Medicis until 1743. When the last member of the dynasty, Gian Gastone, died, the duchy was transferred to Francis I of Lorraine, the husband of Empress Maria Theresa of Austria. The Habsburg-Lorraines governed Tuscany until 1859 – with a fifteen-year interruption between 1799 and 1814, when the French, Napoleon's sister Elisa among them, ruled Florence and held court in the city.

In 1859, Grand Duke Leopold II was expelled from Florence, and in 1860 Tuscany relinquished its century-old

independence in favor of a unified Italy. Florence was the capital of the Kingdom of Italy from 1865 to 1870, until Victor Emmanuel II moved to Rome.

Florence Today

During the Second World War, Florence was devastated by Allied bombing raids and by the German troops who destroyed all of the bridges over the Arno when they retreated in 1944 – with the sole exception of the Ponte Vecchio.

During the catastrophic floods of November 4, 1966, when the Arno River rose with extreme rapidity to 5.2 meters above its normal level, many precious works of art were damaged or destroyed. The people of Florence pitched in selflessly, aided by countless helpers from all over the country, to save whatever could be saved.

The last major calamity to be suffered by the city was the car bomb that went off in front of the Uffizi Gallery on May 27, 1993, which killed five people and injured 50 others, as well as grievously damaging a number of works of art.

Today, Florence numbers almost half a million inhabitants, and continues to expand upriver along the Arno. In order to protect the old center of the city from the corrosive effects of exhaust fumes, private automobile traffic was banned there in 1988. There are attended parking lots around the edge of the downtown area, as well as on the other side of the Arno. Since most sights are relatively close to one another, they can be reached quite comfortably on foot.

A tip to aid in orientation: Florence's system of house numbering can be, to say the least, confusing. Shops and restaurants have red house numbers (the address includes a red "R"), while private residences and hotels have black ones. The red and the black are two independent series of consecutive numbers.

And another tip: Watch out for pickpockets and purse snatchers! Don't carry your purse on the street side. Be alert when you are in large groups, especially

when groups of gypsy women or children come begging and you are jolted or pushed. This is meant to distract you for a minute, and after they have passed by, you may well find that your wallet has disappeared.

The City

For a first view out over the city of Florence, drive up the beautiful winding road to the **Piazzale Michelangelo ❶**, which was built for this very purpose by Guiseppe Poggi between the years 1867 and 1875.

Located 50 meters above the city on the south side of the Arno, the square offers a spectacular view which takes in the palaces, the towers, the dominating dome of Brunelleschi, the hills which enclose everything on three sides, the river flowing westward to the plain and its bridges. The

Above: World-famous designs from a couple of different centuries. Right: Juggler on the Piazza del Duomo.

view is particularly stunning at sunset, when the sky goes a soft bluish green and the first lights start to come on in the city below.

If you want to avoid the inevitable crowds of tourists thronging this observation terrace, take a stroll over to the Forte di Belvedere at a slightly higher elevation, where the view is just as spectacular – if not more so – but the crowds are smaller. As a bonus, from here you can even see the hilly landscape of the Chianti region to the south.

When you have drunk your fill of this picturesque view of the Duomo, the Campanile, the towers of the Palazzo Vecchio and Badia, Orsanmichele, Santa Maria Novella and Santa Croce – to name just a few of the most impressive sights – clothe yourself in equanimity and patience and plunge into the crowds of tourists that choke the streets of Florence from March to October. Florence, after all, has an enormous number of works of art – only Rome has more – in a very small area. If you keep you eyes open, however, and dare to venture into the little side streets away from the main tourist routes, you can still experience a taste of of the city's real Italian ambience.

*Duomo (Cathedral), Campanile and **Baptistery

These three monuments form the spiritual center of the city. They are located on a narrow space which had to be cleared by hand before they could be built. Perhaps the best place from which to get a full view of them is the **Loggia del Bigallo**, located between the Via dei Calzaiuoli and the Via Roma, which was built in the 14th century as the seat of the *Misericordia*, a charitable institution that is still in operation today.

The Duomo, *****Santa Maria del Fiore** ❷, was begun in 1296. Arnolfo di Cambio, the architect, situated it where the Santa Reparata church used to stand (remains of which can be seen inside the present edifice). After Di Cambio's death, the work was continued by the best architects of the time (Giotto, Andrea Pisano, Francesco Talenti and Giovanni Ghini) and finally completed with the construction of the dome in 1436. Building the dome was perhaps the greatest challenge ever faced by the architect Brunelleschi. He determined to build it without using scaffolding, tile by tile, and working from the outside in. Technically this was an enormously difficult undertaking, which was finally completed in the face of every conceivable kind of obstacle. After Brunelleschi's death, Michelozzo constructed the lantern according to Brunelleschi's design, while Verrocchio topped it off with the golden ball you see today. Cracks were recently discovered in the roof of the dome, but these were probably there right from the start.

The outer walls of the Cathedral are encased in marble; green from Prato, white from Carrara and red from the Maremma. The intricate and somewhat overelabo-

rate façade, decorated with figures, was not created until the 19th century. The gloomy, stark interior of the Cathedral covers an area of 8,300 square meters and can accommodate up to 25,000 people. Interesting features are the clock above the main door, of which the hands run counter-clockwise; the canonical sacristy with a terra-cotta *Ascension* by Luca della Robbia over the door; the New Sacristy with its bronze door by Michelozzo and Maso di Bartolomeo, through which Lorenzo the Magnificent fled from the assassins of the Pazzi Conspiracy in 1478; the restored dome painting; and, in the left transept, the metal plate in the floor which has been used for astronomical measurements since the 15th century.

Another notable work of art is an equestrian painting by Paolo Uccello (1436) of Sir John Hawkwood – Giovanni Acuto to the Italians – who was the leader of the English mercenaries who fought alongside the Florentine army at the end of the 14th century. Its complicated perspectives make it an important example

of Renaissance painting. A painting of Dante (on the same wall) standing in front of a medieval Florence is a Florentine tribute to the greatest Italian poet, as well as a gesture of atonement for the fact that he was banished from his home town.

Next to the Cathedral is one of the most magnificent towers in the world, Giotto's **Campanile**. The construction of this Gothic masterpiece, which is almost 85 meters high, was started in 1334. After Giotto's death it was completed by Andrea Pisano and Francesco Talenti between 1336 and 1359.

The base of this fine and seemingly weightless tower is decorated with two rows of bas-reliefs by Andrea Pisano and Luca della Robbia (the originals are on display in the Cathedral Museum). The ogival windows in the tower actually get larger the higher you go up, and convey an almost filigree lightness to the tower.

Above: Gates of Paradise on the Baptistery. Right: The Singer's Pulpit by Luca Della Robbia in the Cathedral Museum (detail).

From its top, which you reach after climbing 414 steps, there is an impressive view of the dome of the Cathedral and the surrounding buildings.

The ****Baptistery ❸**, like the Duomo and the Campanile, is clad with polychrome marble and is one of the oldest buildings in Florence. There is still some dispute as to exactly when *Il bel San Giovanni* – as Dante referred to the church where he was baptized – was built. It is assumed that its structure dates from the 11th or 12th century, and that it was erected on the site of an older building from the 4th to the 6th century. The octagonal church, which is reminiscent of ancient Roman buildings, is crowned by an eight-sided white pyramidal roof which conceals the cupola beneath it. The interior of the cupola is lined with magnificent mosaics representing the medieval concept of Heaven, Hell and Purgatory. The the tomb of the antipope John XXIII, which was designed jointly by Donatello (Donato di Niccolò di Betto Bardi) and Michelozzo around the year 1425, is noteworthy.

The most beautiful aspect of the Baptistery is, however, the three famous bronze doors which are a highlight of Western sculpture. The **South Door**, oldest of the three, was created by Andrea Pisano and for us represents the sunset of Gothic sculpture in Florence. The **North Door** was started by Lorenzo Ghiberti seven years later, following a competition in which his proposed design was selected over those of Brunelleschi and Jacopo della Quercia. It took 21 years to complete this work, executed with the participation of such other great artists as Masolino, Donatello, Uccello and Michelozzo. The **East Door**, or **Gates of Paradise**, which faces the Cathedral, was Ghiberti's masterpiece. He started it in 1425 and took 27 years to complete it. "It was executed with great patience and effort. Of all my works it is the most remarkable... it was executed with great

skill, in the right proportions and with understanding," he said himself of it. In fact, these relief panels depicting scenes from the Old Testament, with rich architectural and natural backgrounds, demonstrate both exact perspective and a truly lifelike quality. In his work the artist included a portrait of himself to be preserved for posterity (left-hand door, right-hand side, fourth head from the top). The panels containing the reliefs are gradually being restored and replaced by copies. The originals are in the Cathedral Museum.

The **Cathedral Museum** is located at the rear of the Duomo, across from the apse. It contains works of art from the Duomo, the Baptistery and the Campanile which are stored here to protect them from decay. Artistic highlights include the two choir-gallery pulpits by Luca della Robbia and Donatello; the *Pietà* by Michelangelo, which he started when he was already of advanced age and which was completed by his student Calcagni; and Donatello's wood carving of Mary Magdalene.

From the Piazza Duomo to the Signoria

From the Piazza Duomo, the Via de' Calzaioli, lined with elegant shops, leads to the Piazza della Signoria. Halfway along, the Via degli Speziali turns off to the right to the **Piazza della Repubblica**, a large square that occupies the site of the Roman forum and for which the Mercato Vecchio and countless historical buildings were ruthlessly demolished towards the end of the last century. Only the attractive old cafés that surround the square are really worth visiting here.

A few steps more will bring you to the peculiar church of **Orsanmichele** ❹ (the abbreviation for *San Michele in Orto*), which was originally a granary built in the 13th century by Arnolfo di Cambio in place of an oratory for St. Michael. But a painting alleged to work miracles attracted so many worshipers that the grain was first moved to be stored in one of the upper floors, and finally the whole building was converted into a church. The inte-

rior includes the famous marble taberna-cle of the *Madonna delle Grazie* by Andrea Orcagna, on which lovely reliefs illustrate the life of Mary. Of particular interest on the outside of the building are the pilasters with canopied niches containing the statues of the patron saints of the guilds. Fourteen niches or tabernacles are distributed around the building like a kind of outdoor museum of first-rate Renaissance sculptures, some of which have been replaced by newer works over the years.

*Piazza della Signoria

Signoria means rule or power, and the *Piazza della Signoria ⑤ was and still is the political center of the city. It was the site of the first public assemblies, and it was where the Dominican monk

Above and right: Ammanati's Neptune on the Piazza della Signoria may not be to everyone's taste – but all are agreed about Michelangelo's David.

Savonarola was hanged and then burnt at the stake (a small granite plaque next to the Neptune Fountain commemorates him). The Palazzo Vecchio was originally the residence of the city's councils and administrative offices; then the residence of Duke Cosimo I de' Medici, and from 1865-1971 first the Parliament and the Foreign Ministry of the Kingdom of Italy, and later the seat of the municipal government and residence of the mayor.

The different names the palace has been given over the years reflect the course of the city's history. Originally it was called the Palazzo dei Priori; at the time of the oligarchy it was called the Palazzo della Signoria; when Cosimo I resided there, it was the Palazzo Ducale; and finally, when the duke moved to the Palazzo Pitti, it assumed the name of **Palazzo Vecchio**, the Old Palace.

It is the largest communal palace in Florence (designed by Arnolfo di Cambio in 1298), a forbidding, fortress-like building of irregular blocks of rough-hewn, light brown ashlar, and crowned by the rectangular battlements of the Guelphs. The 94-meter tower with the swallow-tail crenellations of the Ghibellines and steep bronze roof rises high above the Palazzo. It is no accident that the City Hall resembles a fortress: its original purpose really was to protect the civil servants and defend their independence and autonomy.

For the same, defensive reasons, the entrance gate on the west side was kept small. It leads into the courtyard, which is surrounded by high porticos. In the center is a fountain with putti and dolphin by Verrocchio. Not all sections of the Palazzo's interior are open to the public. Most of the rooms date back to the 16th century and are decorated with numerous frescoes, paintings and statues.

The Piazza della Signoria resembles an open-air sculpture museum. Michelangelo's *David* takes pride of place in front of the main entrance to City Hall, although what you see here is a copy (the

original, which was created between 1501 and 1504, is on display in the Galleria dell'Accademia). The Florentines claimed that this work represented the victory of democracy over tyranny. Opposite stands the marble group *Hercules and Cacus* by Bandinelli (1533), which Cellini is said to have described as resembling a sack full of pumpkins.

The *Marzocco Lion* (which derives its name from the fact that the lion is said to have once stood at the plinth of a column of Mars) with the coat-of-arms of Florence is the emblem of the city; it is modeled on a sandstone original by Donatello (now in the Bargello). Defeated enemies of the Florentines supposedly had to kiss the lion's hindquarters. In 1980, a copy of Donatello's bronze sculpture of *Judith and Holofernes* was placed alongside it.

In the southwest corner of the Palazzo is the Neptune Fountain, with its sea-god by Ammanati, which is said to have inspired the following remark from his contemporaries: *"Ammanato, Ammanato, che bel marmo hai rovinato!"* ("...what

beautiful marble you have ruined!"). The equestrian statue (1594-1598) to the left of the fountain is by Giambologna and represents Cosimo I. The reliefs in the plinth depict him being crowned archduke by Pope Pius V.

On the southern edge of the piazza is the **Loggia dei Lanzi**, built between 1376 and 1382 by Benci di Cione and Simone Talenti, probably based on a design by Orcagna. It was named after the German mercenaries (*Landsknechte*, or *lanzichenecchi*) who acted as guards here for Duke Alessandro I de' Medici. Today, the loggia houses a collection of statues, among them the famous sculpture *Perseus and the Head of Medusa* by Benvenuto Cellini (around 1550).

**Uffizi

To the left of the Loggia dei Lanzi, which served as an architectural model for the Feldherrnhalle in Munich, we continue on to the **Uffizi ❻, the former "offices" of the archducal administration,

located between the Palazzo Vecchio and the Arno. Vasari built this edifice between 1560 and 1574, and it houses one of the richest museums in the world. Famous masterpieces include works by Botticelli (*The Birth of Venus, The Allegory of Spring, The Adoration of the Magi*), Piero della Francesca (*The Duke of Urbino*), Filippo Lippi (images of the Madonna), Michelangelo (*The Holy Family*), Raphael (*The Madonna of the Goldfinch*), Titian (*The Venus of Urbino*), Mantegna (*The Adoration of the Magi*), and so many others that it would take much more than just one visit to see them all.

The two parallel sections of the Uffizi building are connected by an open loggia on the south side. A corridor, built by Vasari in 1565, leads from the Uffizi across the Ponte Vecchio to the Palazzo Pitti, thus ensuring a private, safe and discreet connection between the two build-

ings. This has been accessible to visitors since 1997.

Bargello and Santa Croce

Passing the memorial to Cosimo I, continue on through the Via de' Gondi to Piazza San Firenze. At the far end of this piazza is the **Palazzo del Podestà** or **Bargello** ❼. This plain battlemented castle, a symbol of the victory of Florence's bourgeoisie over the squabbling aristocracy, was begun in 1255, half a century before the Palazzo Vecchio, and is therefore the oldest secular building in Florence. It started out as the official seat of the city leader, then of the *podestà* (city government), and finally became a courthouse and prison (*bargello* = police captain). Today, it contains the National Museum, and is therefore home to the best collection of Florentine Renaissance sculptures in existence.

The impressive interior courtyard (14th century) has a circular arcade and a magnificent flight of steps leading up to a

Above: Botticelli's "Spring" alone is worth a visit to the Uffizzi. Right: Open-air staircase in the inner courtyard of the Bargello.

loggia. Right next to the octagonal fountain in the courtyard stood the arena for public executions, until Grand Duke Leopold abolished the death penalty in 1782.

Across from the Bargello is the **Badia** ❽; this building's pointed tower is a memorable characteristic of the skyline of Florence. This church, a part of the oldest and most important monastery in the city dating from the 10th century, has frequently been extended and rebuilt over the course of the centuries. Inside there are a number of works of art, among them a masterpiece by Filippo Lippi and the tomb of the Tuscan Margrave Ugo (d. 1001) by Mino da Fiesole. The atmospheric cloister is called *Chiostro degli Aranci* (Cloister of the Orange Trees).

Right next to the Badia is Via Dante Alighieri and the **Casa di Dante**, the house where Dante is said to have been born. Within the building various mementoes commemorating the greatest Italian poet are displayed.

The Via dell'Anguillara leads to the Franciscan church of Santa Croce and the **Piazza Santa Croce**, one of the most attractive squares in Florence, lined with old mansions and palaces. It is here that the traditional *Calcio in Costume*, a historical football match between the city's different *quartieri*, takes place every year in June.

Santa Croce ❾ is the largest and most beautiful of the Franciscan churches. It was begun in 1294, possibly by Arnolfo di Cambio, and was finally consecrated in 1443. The polychrome marble façade and the Neo-Gothic campanile were added to this Gothic church during the 19th century. The cruciform interior is a kind of pantheon of Florentine notables: the mendicant monks required financial support for its construction, and the return for a pious contribution was a final resting place within the walls of the church itself. Here you will find tombs or monuments to such men of genius as Michelangelo,

Around Florence

Dante, Machiavelli, Foscolo, Rossini, Alberti, Cherubini, Galileo Galilei, and many others.

Even more striking than the tombs themselves are the works of art that were donated by the families of the deceased. Standing out among them in particular are Donatello's relief of the Annunciation and his famous wooden crucifix, of which Brunelleschi is said to have remarked that it looked as if the artist had nailed a peasant to the cross. Then there are Rosselino's *Madonna and Child*, the octagonal marble pulpit by Benedetto da Maiano, and frescoes by Maso, Taddeo Gaddi and Giotto. Coincidentally, one may note that the church of Santa Croce houses the largest organ in Italy.

To the right of the church, in Santa Croce's first cloister, Brunelleschi created one of the very first Renaissance buildings, the **Pazzi Chapel**. The Museum of Santa Croce is located in the former refectory of the monastery and adjacent rooms, and contains a collection of masterpieces of Florentine art.

South of the monastery of Santa Croce is a huge complex that extends down to the Arno, the **Biblioteca Nazionale** ⑩. Built at the beginning of the 20th century, it houses a vast collection of manuscripts, incunabula, drawings and prints from the collections of the Medici, the Palatine Electors and the Lorraines. Since 1885, a copy of every book published in Italy has been deposited here. The catastrophic flood of 1966 severely damaged innumerable objects both in the National Library and in Santa Croce.

*San Marco

San Marco, another Dominican monastery in Florence, is situated on the piazza of the same name, which you can reach by Via Cavour or Via Ricasoli from the Cathedral square. If you opt for Via Ricasoli, you will see, on the right just be-

Above: Santa Maria Novella. Right: The Accademia offers plenty of material for aspiring artists.

fore you come to the Piazza San Marco, the *★Galleria dell'Accademia* ⑪, which since 1910 has housed the original sculpture of David, as well as other works by Michelangelo.

The monastery of ★**San Marco** ⑫ was built by Michelozzo for Cosimo the Elder from 1437 to 1452. The monks' cells on the upper floor are today a Fra Angelico museum: this is where the "Blessed" Fra Angelico painted frescoes on the walls of his fellow monks' cells to inspire them to meditate. The most famous fresco, **The Annunciation**, is at the staircase leading to the first floor. At the far end of the right corridor are the cells that belonged to Savonarola when he was the prior of the monastery. A large bell by Donatello, the *Piagnona* or Bell of Lamentation, is set up in the cloister. It was rung to assemble the followers of this hyper-moral monk, whose aim was to turn all of Florence into a monastery. After his execution the bell was temporarily removed so that its sound would no longer remind people of this unpopular reformer.

Besides the frescoes in the cells, San Marco contains other famous paintings by the blessed Fra Angelico, such as the *Descent from the Cross* and the famous *Tabernacle of the Linaioli* (the flax-workers) in the pilgrims' hospice, it also displays a *Last Supper* by Ghirlandaio in the refectory, as well as works by Fra Bartolomeo. The library, which was also built by Michelozzo, contains precious manuscripts, missals and bibles, some of which are on display.

A painting of the Last Supper of great artistic value can be seen in the monastery of ★**Sant'Apollonia** ⑬ at Via XXVII Aprile No. 1, to the west of Piazza San Marco. In the refectory of the former Benedictine monastery there is a museum containing works by the Renaissance painter Andrea del Castagno, including his *Last Supper*; this painting is captivating because of its realism, exact perspectives and powerful presentation.

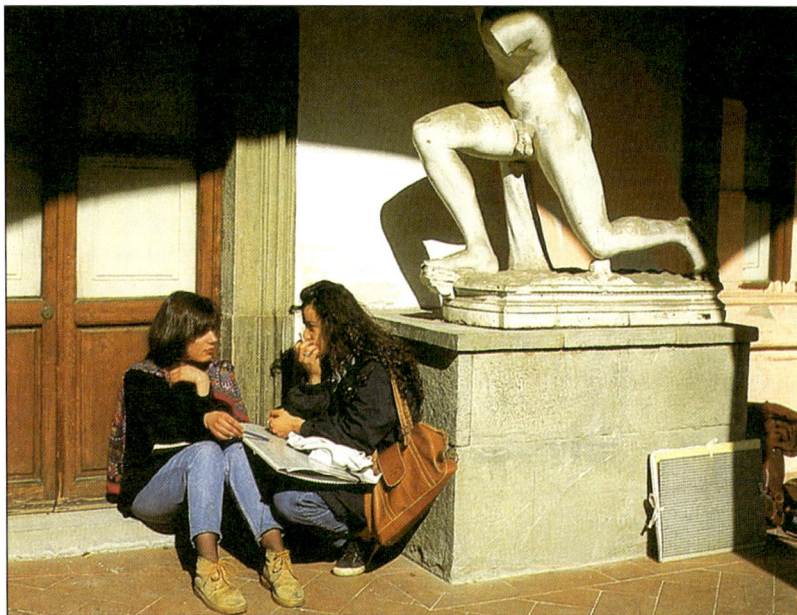

Santisima Annunziata and ** San Lorenzo

Continuing along the Via Battisti, you come, after a short walk, to the **Piazza della Santissima Annunziata** ⑭, a broad square surrounded by stately loggias. The equestrian statue of Ferdinand I in the center of the piazza is Giambologna's last work and was completed by Tacca, who also created the two curious fountains.

What is most impressive about this harmonious piazza, which resembles a huge cloister, is Brunelleschi's 15th-century façade of the **Ospedale degli Innocenti** (Foundlings' Hospital), with its resplendent loggia and the charming majolica reliefs of terra-cotta babes in swaddling clothes by the great Andrea della Robbia.

One hundred years later, Antonio da Sangallo and Baccio d'Agnolo created the portico for the Servite Order on the opposite side of the square, and at the end of the 16th century the piazza was rounded off with the portico of the **Basil-ica of Santissima Annunziata** on the north side. A few steps beyond Piazza Santissima Annunziata, on Via della Colonna, is the entrance to the **Archeological Museum** in the Palazzo Crocetta. The museum – unjustly neglected by most visitors to Florence – contains Greek and Etruscan masterpieces, which can provide good insight into the art of ancient times.

Continue along the Via dei Servi in the direction of the Duomo to Via dei Pucci, the extension of which is Via de Gori, which leads right to Piazza San Lorenzo. At the corner opposite the San Lorenzo Church is the **Palazzo Medici-Riccardi** ⑮, which Michelozzo built for Cosimo the Elder in the 15th century. The great palace, built of solid blocks of ashlar and with iron grilles over the windows on the ground floor, looks more like a fortress than the city residence of a wealthy family. Today the Palazzo houses a Medici museum. In the house chapel on the upper floor you can see precious frescoes by Benozzo Gozzoli.

The church of **San Lorenzo** ⑯, commissioned by the Medici family, was built by Brunelleschi on a structure from the 4th century that had been destroyed by fire. Michelangelo's design for the facing of the brick façade was never carried out. The interior of this triple-naved church projects an air of harmony, calmness and serenity. The rich decor, of great artistic note, includes two bronze pulpits by Donatello as well as one of the most important works of Filippo Lippi, *The Annunciation* (over the altar).

The **Old Sacristy** (enter from the left-hand transept) is by Brunelleschi. In its architectonic perfection, it became a model for the ideals of European architecture. The interior was decorated by Donatello and contains a tomb and a sarcophagus for members of the Medici family, both works of Verrocchio (1472). The cloister is a picturesque garden court

Above: Images of foundlings on the loggia of the Ospedale degli Innocenti. Right: The market hall of San Lorenzo.

which leads to the renowned **Biblioteca Laurenziana** by Michelangelo, which contains one of the most comprehensive collections of manuscripts in the world.

You can reach the **Medici Chapel** and the **New Sacristy** from the Piazza Madonna degli Aldobrandini. The octagonal **Medici Chapel** (1604) serves as a funerary chapel for six Medici princes. It is imposing, austere and cold, unlike the **New Sacristy**, a funerary chapel built for the Medici family by Michelangelo, which also contains his famous tombs. This masterpiece of the High Renaissance manages ingeniously to combine sculpture and architecture. The two tombs which were actually realized – Michelangelo had originally projected six – rise up from the wall which, with its strict lines and clear geometric divisions, has an almost three-dimensional effect. Within the tombs Lorenzo II, grandson of Lorenzo the Magnificent, and Giuliano, one of his sons, are interred. In niches above the tombs stand statues of the dead, while resting atop the sarcophagi themselves

are the allegorical figures of Dawn and Dusk, Day and Night.

On the Piazza San Lorenzo, and spilling over into the alleys around it, there's a colorful street market. It is, unfortunately, rather heavily geared towards tourists, so locals frequent the **Mercato Centrale di San Lorenzo** ⑰, the great market hall whose two floors are also a mecca for Florentine gourmets. The ironwork construction of this 19th-century building is reminiscent of Parisian train stations and is definitely worth a look. The colorful stalls are a feast for the eye and the unbelievably varied selection of edibles is sure to make your mouth water.

And speaking of food, try one of the simple restaurants behind the market hall if you want to have a really good lunch. These eateries have small kitchens staffed by perspiring cooks, and rather limited menus offering only one or two simple dishes; but what you get is likely to represent the very best of plain Florentine fare. Some of these places tend to be rather crowded, and you may have to wait a

while for a table, but your patience will generally be rewarded.

Art connoisseurs will find a special treat near San Lorenzo in the refectory of the former Franciscan monastery of **★San Onofrio** ⑱ at Via Faenza 42: *The Last Supper* by Perugino. Painted by the artist in 1445-1450, this is one of the most famous depictions of the Last Supper in all of Florence.

★Santa Maria Novella

The second church of a mendicant order in Florence is **★Santa Maria Novella** ⑲, situated near the train station (which bears its name). This mighty building dominates the Piazza Santa Maria Novella, to clear space for which the city bought up a number of old buildings and then had them demolished. The church was constructed in 1279, the façade – the lower part of which is Romanesque-Gothic – was finally completed in the 15th century in the Renaissance style by Leon Battisti Alberti.

The triple-naved interior is a masterpiece of the Florentine Gothic style. The side altars accommodate the graves of notable Florentines, and are decorated with paintings and frescoes. The famous fresco of the *Trinity* by Masaccio in the left nave was discovered in the 19th century behind an altar with a painting by Vasari. The fresco is organized according to strictly applied rules of perspective, and reflects the new concept of the importance of man that was central to the philosophy of the early Renaissance; the portraits of donors at the sides of the painting are on the same scale as the holy figures, rather than on a smaller scale, as they would have been in the Middle Ages to reflect their lesser importance.

The frescoes in the choir, executed by Domenico Ghirlandaio, represent the

Above: Feel free to touch – the bronze boar as a symbol of good luck. Right: From shoemaker to millionaire – a shoe museum in the Palazzo Feroni (Piazza Santa Trinità) is dedicated to Salvatore Ferragamo.

people, customs and taste of the period in a precise yet carefree manner. They are thus an invaluable document which allows insights into, for example, life in the home of an aristocratic family at the time of Lorenzo the Magnificent (fresco of the *Birth of Mary* on the left wall).

The celebrated crucifix carved by Brunelleschi stands on the altar of the Gondi Chapel, which Donatello unselfishly praised as being much more beautiful than his own crucifix in Santa Croce. Another masterpiece is the painted crucifix by Giotto in the sacristy.

To the right of the church is an old cemetery where members of leading Florentine families are buried. To the left of this is the entrance to the cloisters of the former Dominican monastery. The first of these, the so-called Green Cloister, derives its name from the various shades of green on its walls in the shady figures which are all that has survived of Paolo Uccello's frescoes of the story of the Creation. But you can still make out the images of some of the episodes they

represent; those of *The Deluge* and *Noah's Sacrifice* are especially striking.

In the Spanish Chapel there are impressive 14th-century frescoes by Andrea da Firenze depicting the missionary works and triumphs of the Dominican Order. People are represented as sheep, guarded by black and white dogs – *domini canes*, "dogs of God," or Dominicans – while the wolves being torn apart by the dogs represent the heretics (Cathars and Waldensians) who enjoyed a considerable following in Florence at that time.

The Right Bank of the Arno

From the Piazza della Signoria, continue on westwards through the Via Vacchereccia to the **Loggia del Mercato Nuovo** ㉔ (16th century), where gold and silk merchants used to meet. Today, it's a great place for anyone looking to purchase samples of Florentine artisanship. On the south side of the loggia is the famous **Fontana del Porcellino** by Tacca (early 17th century). The "piglet" is actu-

ally a full-grown bronze wild boar which replaced a marble original in the Uffizi. Touching it and throwing a coin into the fountain are supposed to bring good luck. The brightly polished bronze of the statue's snout indicate that many people give it a try.

Not far from here, on the Via Porta Rossa, is the **Palazzo Davanzati** ㉑, where the Museum of the Old Florentine House has been located since 1956. The collection of furniture and objects for everyday use from the Middle Ages, the Renaissance and the Baroque period provide an interesting look into the highly civilized life of Florence's middle classes, and the precious furnishings of their homes.

Continue on to Via Tornabuoni, one of Florence's most attractive and elegant streets, and the **Piazza Santa Trinità** ㉒, with a church of the same name. The column which supports the statue of Justice by Tadda (16th century) is a granite monolith that originally stood in the Baths of Caracalla in Rome.

The Gothic church of **Santa Trinità**, which dates back to the 11th century, was extended in the 13th and 14th centuries, and fitted out with a Baroque façade by Buontalenti in 1593-1594. The fine interior was financed by aristocratic families who had built their palaces nearby; two of these *palazzi*, in fact, are located directly on this piazza.

Better known than either of these, however, is the **Palazzo Strozzi** ㉓, which stands a little further away on the corner of Via Tornabuoni and Via Strozzo. Filippo Strozzi had it built by Benedetto da Maiano in 1489, and it was completed in 1536 by Cronaca. Legend has it that the wealthy merchant Strozzi did not want to upset the most powerful man in Florence, Lorenzo the Magnificent, by building this opulent city palace. He therefore had a rumor spread to the effect that he was putting shops in on the ground floor to

Above and right: The Ponte Vecchio, Florence's most famous bridge. Here, only goldsmiths' shops are allowed.

finance the expensive building with the rents. Lorenzo was dismayed at the idea of his beautiful city being thus disfigured, and quickly granted Strozzi a free hand in building his palace. The result was one of the loveliest Renaissance palaces in Florence. Today, it is home to various scientific institutions, and sometimes hosts major exhibitions.

If you continue on towards the Arno along the Via Tornabuoni, you will come across one of Florence's most attractive bridges, the **Ponte Santa Trinità** ㉔. The bridge (1567-70) was blown up by the retreating German Army in 1944, but then rebuilt from the rubble retrieved from the Arno. Thus Ammanati's masterpiece, which was based on a design by Michelangelo, was preserved.

Strolling further down the Arno, you'll pass the **Palazzo Corsini** ㉕, with its splendid private collection of paintings (the entrance is on the Via del Parione), and come to the Piazza Goldoni. Here, the Via della Vigna Nuova turns off sharply to the right. On the left side of the

street is the palace and the chapel of the Rucellai family, both designed by Leon Battista Alberti. Also starting at the Piazza Goldoni is the Borgo Ognissanti, which will bring you to the square of the same name and the church of **Ognissanti** 26 (Church of All Saints). Founded during the 13th century, it was remodeled in 1627 by Bartolomeo Pettirossi into the first Baroque church in Florence. It contains important works of art, in particular the *Madonna* by Domenico and Davide Ghirlandaio, *The Last Supper* by Domenico Ghirlandaio (in the refectory), *Saint Augustine in his Study* by Botticelli, and a *Saint Jerome* by Ghirlandaio.

In contrast to the Baroque Ognissanti, the **Ospedale San Giovanni di Dio**, which is situated nearby, probably dates back all the way to the 14th century.

Across the ★Ponte Vecchio to the Left Bank of the Arno

The ★**Ponte Vecchio** 27 is the oldest and most famous bridge in Florence. It is very likely that the Etruscans built a bridge at this point over the Arno; and it's certain that the Romans did. When the German Army was retreating from the city in 1944, Hitler ordered that all bridges over the Arno be blown up. Yet the Ponte Vecchio was spared, thanks to a brave officer who dared to disobey orders and, rather than blowing up the bridge, simply blew up the houses at either end to block access. Thus this masterpiece was saved for posterity.

In the Middle Ages, it was the butchers who had their shops on the bridge, from which they threw their waste directly into the Arno. In 1539, however, Grand Duke Ferdinand passed an ordinance that only goldsmiths were to be allowed to operate shops on the bridge – and so it has remained to this day.

In the center of the bridge, between the two rows of shops, there is an open terrace from which you have a beautiful view of the Arno, Florence and the surrounding hills. On the right side the goldsmiths have erected a bust of Benvenuto

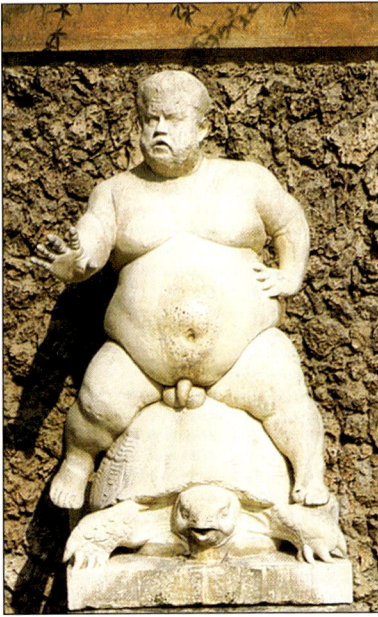

Cellini (1900), one of Florence's most celebrated goldsmiths.

Above the left-hand row of shops runs the enclosed walkway which Vasari built for Cosimo I so that he could move freely between the Palazzo Vecchio and the Uffizi and his residence in the Palazzo Pitti, unobserved by his subjects.

Before turning to the palace itself, turn right and walk parallel to the river until you come to the **Piazza Santo Spirito** ㉘ and the church of Santo Spirito, which Brunelleschi designed for rich Florentine families in 1428. In the course of construction, which continued until the end of the century, the design underwent many changes.

From outside, the church seems rather plain; in fact, its façade was an addition from the 18th century. The triple-naved interior, however, with its semicircular side chapels and Corinthian columns,

Above: Always popular with photographers – the Bachhus in the Boboli Gardens. Right: Interior of San Miniato al Monte.

makes Santo Spirito one of the most brilliant creations of the Florentine Renaissance. This church, like most of the other major churches, also contains many famous works of art, including pieces by Filippino Lippi (*Madonna and Child with Saints and Donors*), Perugino (rose window on the façade) and Giuliano da Sangallo (entry hall and sacristy).

Somewhat further on, along the Via S. Agostino and Via S. Monaca, you'll come to the church of **Santa Maria del Carmine** ㉙, which was leveled by fire in 1771 and rebuilt in the Late Baroque style. Luckily, the ****Brancacci Chapel** in the right transept was spared by the flames, preserving the sublime frescoes by Masaccio (*The Tribute Money*) and his teacher Masolino. The frescoes were started during the 15th century and completed by Filippino Lippi.

The neighborhoods of Santo Spirito and San Frediano, where these two churches are located, are two old, homey quarters where there are still plenty of artisan workshops that produce and restore paintings, furniture and musical instruments, as well as executing a number of other typical Florentine crafts.

*Palazzo Pitti and the
*Boboli Gardens

The Via de Serragli, which divides these two neighborhoods, leads south from the Arno, past the Giardino Torrigiano, to the **Porta Romana**, one of Florence's medieval gates, through which you leave Florence to reach Siena and Rome. From here you can walk back to the Ponte Vecchio along the Via Romana, which is lined with magnificent palaces.

Opening out after Piazza Santa Felice is the gradual upward incline of Piazza Pitti, which is dominated by the imposing ***Palazzo Pitti** ㉚. The palace is 200 meters long and is built entirely of ashlar blocks. Brunelleschi designed it, and construction began in the mid-15th century.

The original client was the wealthy merchant Luca Pitti, but eventually Cosimo I chose it as his residence. Later, when Italy had become a kingdom, Victor Emmanuel II moved in, and in 1919, Victor Emmanuel III bequeathed it and its contents to the state.

The Palazzo Pitti contains one of the most famous collections of paintings in the world, the Galleria Palatina, as well as the Museo degli Argenti, the Museum of Crafts, a collection of costumes from various epochs, magnificently decorated apartments with paintings, tapestries and precious furniture, and the Galleria d'Arte Moderna, which contains art and objects from the 18th and 19th centuries. Ammanati's great courtyard behind the palace was originally used as an impressive open-air stage; and performances are still occasionally put on here today.

On the hill behind the palazzo, Cosimo I laid out the grandiose ***Boboli Gardens** ③. Winding, shaded paths lead up to terraces from which one has a beautiful view out over Florence. Fountains, grottoes, statues and a coffee house (from 1776) make the gardens into a kind of open-air museum. Logically enough, therefore, an admission charge has recently been introduced for visitors (however, you can still walk in the large popular park of **Le Cascine** on the other side of the Arno, west of the train station, free of charge).

On the other side of the Boboli Gardens is the **Forte di Belvedere** ③, a beautifully-renovated fortress built by Buontalenti for Ferdinand I during the 16th century. From the fortress walls (which themselves house major exhibitions) you can also enjoy a stunning panoramic view of Florence and the hills behind the city.

****San Miniato al Monte**

The classic beauty of the Romanesque marble façade of ****San Miniato al Monte** ③ can be seen from all over the

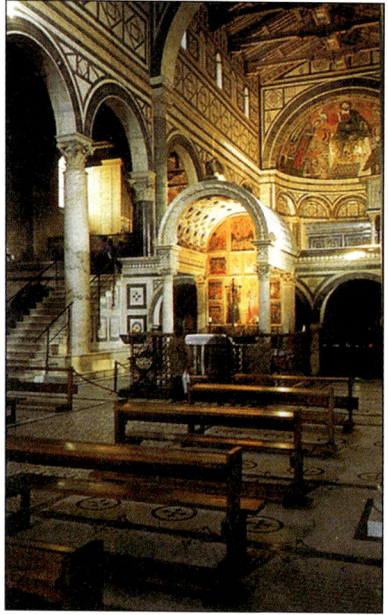

city. St. Minias' first church was established during the reign of Charlemagne, and that monarch bequeathed vast estates to it. Eventually, however, it fell into a state of disrepair, to be built anew in the 11th century.

San Miniato and its baptistery are the most precious examples of Romanesque architecture in Florence. The interior, like the façade, is also decorated with colorful marble; geometric patterns predominate in this beautifully clear space. The raised presbytery with beautiful choir screens stands on a crypt where, within an altar from the 11th century, the bones of St. Minias are kept. In front of this there is a tabernacle by Michelozzo. Note the wonderful inlaid marble floor of the church and the exquisite marble pulpit from the 13th century. To the right of the church is the Episcopal Palace, formerly the summer residence of Florence's bishops. From the square in front of the church you have a beautiful view of the city, which is actually preferable to that from the crowded Piazzale Michelangelo.

Shopping in Florence

Florence is not only a paradise for lovers of art and culture, but also for all who enjoy shopping – and it has something for every preference.

The city center, between the railway station, the Cathedral, the Piazza della Signoria and the Piazza Goldoni, is mainly dedicated to fashion. The Via Tornabuoni and the Via della Vigna Nuova are the domain of the great couturiers: we'll start on the Via Tornabuoni (No. 14r) with **Salvatore Ferragamo** in the Palazzo Feroni-Spini. Salvatore's passion was hand-made shoes which he created for Hollywood stars in the 1920's. The family business is managed today by his wife and children.

Directly opposite (No. 13/15r), the house of **Gianni Versace** presents its collection. Then there are the fashion houses of **Trussardi** (36r), **Bulgari** (61r), **Prada** (67r), **Gucci** (73r) and **Enrico Coveri** (81r). Having reached the Palazzo Strozzi, haute couture fashion continues along the Via della Vigna Nuova towards the Arno: as well as seductive lingerie from **La Perla** (17/19r), modern bags from **Furla** (28r) and ladies' hosiery from **Emilio Cavallini** (24r), the fashion of **Valentino** (47r) and **Giorgio Armani** (51r) is also represented here. **MaxMara**, with an elegant, modern collection for ladies – in a somewhat more moderate but still expensive price range – is situated on Via dei Tornabuoni (No. 80), and also on Via dei Pecori (23r). In **Max & Co.**, the "offspring" of MaxMara on the Via dei Calzaiuoli (89r), the younger generation can find clothing in the latest trends. Business is so good that the collection changes almost every week! Under a painted vaulted ceiling on the Via Calimala (16/18r), **Zini** presents extravagant clothing.

Left: Florence is well known for its beautiful leather fashions and accessories.

For men there is also plenty to choose from in Florence: **Matucci** on the Via del Corso (44/46r) and **Eredi Chiarini Royal** on the Via Roma (16r) both offer wide-ranging fashionable collections. If you prefer a classic style, **Boston Tailor** on the Via Vecchietti (17r) is the right address for you.

How about a beautiful silk necktie and a lambs-wool and silk scarf for him, or an imaginatively patterned silk scarf for her? At **Andrew's Ties** on the Via dei Calzaiuoli (No. 98) and at **Stilnovo** on the Via dei Tavolini (No. 1r) there is a wide selection to choose from.

As far as Italian shoes are concerned, more and more large chains are taking over this sector and driving the smaller shops out of business. Along the Via dei Panzani and Via dei Cerretani, between the station and Cathedral, you will find on the right and left the shops of **Spatafora** (19r) and **Divarese** (49r), where you can purchase Italian shoes suitable for everyday wear. Similar ranges can be found on the "shoe street," the Borgo San Lorenzo: at **Fiorenza**, on the right (No. 30r), the newest fashion for young people, and diagonally opposite, also at Fiorenza (No. 41r), the somewhat cheaper and more classic models. Unfortunately, the shop assistants here are not very friendly.

Marco Candido (No. 5r), to the left of the Cathedral, also has beautiful shoes. On the Via dei Calzaiuoli, which used to be the street of the shoemakers, you will come across the rather special shoes made by **Santini & Dominici** (No. 95r), all of which are flat. The fashionable, somewhat unusual and very comfortable shoes by **Calvani** on the Via Speziali (No. 7r) are popular with young people. At the Piazza della Repubblica, however, you can find classical Italian shoes by **Romano**. Bargain hunters can head to the shops on Via del Corso and the Borgo degli Albizi, where prices are lower.

To continue the theme of leather goods, leather jackets are among the most impor-

tant articles worth purchasing in Florence. If you are prepared to invest in something good, certainly the best place to look is **Noi** on Via delle Terme (No. 8). Here the softest leather is made into fabulous jackets. And the service is both friendly and competent. You can look for cheaper jackets at the San Lorenzo market, where it is a good idea to look around first at what is on offer and then to bargain for the price (prices and quality can vary considerably). Near the church of San Lorenzo there are two stalls where attractive and reasonably priced leather gloves in all possible colors are for sale.

Across the Arno directly after the Ponte Vecchio you can purchase gloves at **Madova Gloves** (No.1r) and, still better, on the Borgo San Jacopo is **Roberta** (No. 74/78r), which also has bags and purses at good prices. The bag shop directly on the

Above: Want to buy some extravagant Holly-wood-style footwear? Salvatore Ferragamo makes it possible. Right: Prêt-à-porter boutique on a Florentine fashion strip.

Piazza San Firenze, behind the Palazzo Vecchio, offers a large selection of good quality bags for ladies and men. For young people the brand name **Mandarina Duck** is held in high esteem. The products are nevertheless fairly expensive. A designer from Parma, **Coccinelle**, shows his collection of bags, which usually have special flair, on Via Por Santa Maria (No. 49r). Mandarina Duck is situated at (No. 23/25r), both are near the Ponte Vecchio. **Nannini** bags, at Via Porta Rossa 64r, on the other hand, sells only products manufactured in Florence.

If your feet are hurting from so much trudging around, you can find everything from hats and clothes to shoes – and many other things besides – all under one roof at **Coin** on the Via dei Calzaiuoli (No. 56r). The mens' department here is excellent. A tour of this exquisite store is well worth while!

For those who are less interested in fashion, a walk *oltrearno* around the district of Santo Spirito, which has maintained much of its traditional character, is

to be recommended. Just beyond the Ponte Vecchio on the Via dei Bardi (No. 17) at **Il Torchio**, you can watch as books, photo albums, etc. are adorned with marbled paper in the most wonderful colors. Or what about a small still life? Between the Ponte Vecchio and Palazzo Pitti you will find **Maria Meriggi**, who paints pictures in the old style. Even more skillful are the small "masterpieces" by **Mario Calzolari** directly opposite. Both shops are in a passage on the right on Via Guicciardini (No. 16).

At **Pitti Mosaici** on the same street (No. 60r) you can find wonderful *pietre dure* inlay work, a traditional Florentine art form (see also p. 82). If you prefer ceramics, have a look at the hand-painted terra-cotta pots at **Il Principe** (No. 110r). **Rosso Fiorentino**, on the other hand, specializes in leather objects: for example, the so-called *tacco fiorentino*, a purse for coins.

On the Via Maggio there is one elegant antique shop after another, among them **Guido Bartolozzi** (No. 18r), a firm of

antique dealers going back many generations. In the district of Santa Croce near the Piazza Ciompi the prices are somewhat lower, but even here there are no bargain prices to be had. **Marcello Chiavacci** is a great lover of antiques who shows his wares in several shops on the Via della Spada (No. 41r).

Would you rather look for a small golden souvenir, so as not to add unnecessarily to the weight of your baggage? At the time of the Renaissance, Florence was already well known for its goldsmiths' work. In the late 16th century the Medici family replaced the butchers' shops on the Ponte Vecchio with goldsmiths' shops which have remained there until the present day. The goldsmiths here generally use 18 carat gold.

What about elegant gold jewelry by **Elisabetta Fallaci** (No. 22), or coral, cameos and pearls from **Gherardi** (No. 5r), or jewelry in the old Florentine style from **Bucelli Maria** (No. 33r)? A little more reasonably priced jewelry can be found at **Linea Punto Oro**, made by

Stefano Ricci. He has his goldsmith's shop in an old palace on the Via Santo Spirito (No. 11). If you prefer silver, you can find natural stones from the sea in plain settings at **Gabriella Nanni** on the Via Lambertesca (No. 28r).

Finally, what about Florence's market life? Italy's most beautiful covered market is situated in Florence, the **Mercato Centrale di San Lorenzo**, dating from the late 19th century, where fruit, vegetables, meat and cheese are on offer like in the Land of Milk and Honey. Apart from the large market at San Lorenzo, which specializes in leather goods and because of its location is mainly visited by tourists, Florence has a variety of other markets, further from the center, where mainly locals purchase their clothes, shoes, etc. At these you may find the occasional bargain.

The largest market, the **Mercato Cascine**, takes place every Tuesday

Above: Not only the cheese stands are well stocked at the Mercato Centrale di S. Lorenzo.

morning in the Cascines district, further down the Arno. Here, there is just about everything on offer – from food to household goods and plants, from hats and gloves to dresses and shoes. At some market stalls you can rummage around a bit, and maybe you'll find a nice sweater or pair of trousers for 20,000 Lire – but you need to watch out here for pickpockets! On the first Sunday of the month a **flea market** takes place on the **Piazza Santo Spirito**, and on every third Sunday of the month there is a "bio-market," where biologically-produced olive oil from Tuscany and whole-grain breads are on offer. On the fourth Sunday of every month there is a large **flea market** on the **Piazza Ciompi**.

So there are more than enough possibilities to lighten up your wallet. If, however, you would rather avoid shopping away your sightseeing savings, there is only one way to do it: devote yourself entirely to the appreciation of the arts, and keep your eyes tightly closed while on the way from one church to the next.

FLORENCE (☎ 055)

𝑖 Tourist Information Office (APT), Via A. Manzoni, 16, tel. 23320, fax 2346286. Internet: www.firenze. turismo.toscana.it. E-mail: apt@firenze.turismo. toscana.it. **Tourist Information at Amerigo Vespucci Airport**, tel. 315874, fax 318609. **City and Province of Florence**, Via Cavour 1r, tel. 290832/3.

🚗 CAR RENTAL: **Avis**, Lungarno Torrigiani 33b, tel. 241145, weekends, Borgo Ognissanti 128, tel. 213629. **Europcar**, Borgo Ognissanti 53, tel. 2360072. **Hertz**, Via Maso Finguerra 23, tel. 2398205. RAIL: Central station **Santa Maria Novella**, Piazza Stazione, tel. 147888088 (9 am-5 pm), 24 hour information, tel. 166-105050.

BUS COMPANIES: **A.T.A.F.** (city bus routes, good services to central train station and Cathedral, tickets from machines at newsstands and in many bars, 24-hour tourist ticket), tel. 5650222. **SITA**, Via Santa Caterina da Siena 15, regional bus routes, tel. 214721, 483651, long distance routes, tel. 294955, 24-hour service, tel. 166845010. **CAP**, Largo Fratelli Alinari 9, tel. 214637.

Tour buses (reservations, tours): Tour buses arrive at the parking areas Olmatello Palazzeschi and Strozzi Montelungo according to a 'bus pass system' between 8/9 am and 8 pm.

BICYCLE RENTAL: **Alinari**, Via Guelfa 85, tel. 280500.

AIRPORT: **Amerigo Vespucci**, Peretola, Via del Termine 11, tel. 373498, domestic flights, tel. 3061700, international flights, tel. 3061702.

RADIO TAXIS: CO.TA.FI tel. 4390, 4499. SO.CO.TA. tel. 4242, 4798.

ATTENDED PARKING: **Fortezza da Basso**, large parking lot near central station. **Central station/Station S.M.N.**, underground parking.

FURTHER PARKING LOTS: Mercato Centrale, Lungarno Torrigiani, Lungarno Zecca Vecchia, Piazza della Libertà, on the circular roads.

🏨 ⓢⓢⓢ **Annalena**, Via Romana 34, tel. 222402, fax 222403, some rooms with view of the Boboli Gardens, near the Pitti Palace, fairly low wooden ceilings everywhere. Breakfast is charged separately. **Excelsior**, Piazza Ognissanti 3, tel. 264201, fax 210278. **Regency**, Piazza M. d'Azeglio 3, tel. 245247, fax 2346735. **Brunelleschi**, Piazza S. Elisabetta 3, tel. 27370, fax 219653. **Minerva**, Piazza S. M. Novella 16, tel. 284555, fax 268281.

ⓢⓢ **Beacci Tornabuoni**, Via Tornabuoni 3, tel. 212645, fax 283594, in the upper floors of a medieval city palace, attractive interior decoration, roof garden for house guests. **Galileo**, Via Nazionale 22/A, tel. 496645, fax 496447. **Golf**, Viale Fratelli Rosselli 56, tel.

281818, fax 268432, often full, even outside of the peak season, parking available in courtyard. **David**, Viale Michelangelo 1, tel. 6811695, fax 680602. **La Noce**, Borgo La Noce 8, tel. 292346, fax 291035, in an old building, but the rooms in the second floor have been refurbished and have TV. Very close to market. **Pendini**, Via Strozzi 2, tel. 211170, fax 281807, in the upper floors of a 19th-century building, room decor in imitation Baroque style, large rooms with a view over the Piazza della Repubblica or else of the rather neglected interior courtyard. **Porta Rossa**, Via Porta Rossa 19, tel. 287551, fax 282179, 14th-century building, renovations during many centuries were made in various styles and are still continuing today, good atmosphere but not always modern comfort for sleeping, reasonably quiet location in a side alley. **Select**, Via Galliano 24, tel. 330342, fax 351506, air-conditioned rooms with bath, mini-bar and TV, garage parking. **Vasari**, Via B. Cennini 9-11, tel. 212753, fax 294246, well-cared-for inn near train station, limited parking in hotel courtyard.

ⓢ **Alessandra**, Borgo SS. Apostoli 17, tel. 283438, fax 210619, fairly central location near the Ponte Vecchio, clean rooms with wooden furniture. **Casci**, near the Cathedral, tel. 211686, fax 239646, under Swiss management, most rooms are on the side where main road is. **Firenze**, Piazza Donati 4, tel. 214203, fax 212370, in the house where Gemma Donati, the wife of Dante Alighieri, was born. Modern rooms, not far from the Cathedral. **Grazia e Griselda**, Via L. Alamanni, tel. 211145, fax 284617, clean rooms, not all the rooms have showers, though. **Il Cestello**, Piazza di Cestello 9, tel. 280632, fax 280631, quiet location, from some rooms there is a view of the Arno; large refurbished rooms. **La Scaletta**, Via Guicciardini 13, tel. 283028, fax 289562, only a stone's throw from the Ponte Vecchio, rooms of varying sizes deliberately decorated in old-fashioned style; there's a lovely view south from the rooftop terrace to the Boboli Gardens. **La Sorelle Bandini**, Piazza Santo Spirito 9, tel. 215308, fax 282761, early reservations are essential as the hotel has only 10 rooms and is often fully booked, in top floors of a palace building from the 15th century in historical surroundings, with views over the roofs of the city. **Monica**, Via Faenza 66, tel. 283804, fax 281706, small inn with a large air-conditioning system, refurbished, rooftop terrace on the second floor. **Porta Faenza**, Via Faenza 77, tel. 284119, fax 210101. **Santa Croce**, Via Bentaccordi 3, tel. 217000, quiet location in a medieval section of the city. Very small rooms.

HOTEL RESERVATION CENTERS: **Consorzio Finestre Sull'Arno**, c/o Hotel Augustus, Vicolo dell'Oro 5, tel. 571740. **Coopal**, Via II Prato 2r, tel. 219525, fax 292192. **Florence Promhotels**, Viale Volta 72, tel. 570481, fax 587189, Internet: www.promhotels.it, e-mail: info@promhotels.it. **Top Quark** Family Hotels/Sun Rays Hotels/Hotel Italiano, Via Trieste 5, tel. 4620080, fax 482288, Internet: www.emmeti.it/topquark, email: topquark.fi@mbox.it.net. **Associazione Gestori Alloggi Privati** (private rooms), Via dei Neri 9, tel./fax 284100. **Agriturismo** (farmhouse holidays) Mugello Alto Mugello Val die Sieve, tel./fax 571948, e-mail: info.sottobosco@flashnet.it.

AGRITURISMO (farmhouse holidays): **La Fattoressa**, Via Volterrana 58, tel. 2048418. **Le Macine**, Viuzzo del Pozzetto 1, tel. 6531089. **II Milione**, Via di Giogoli 12-14 and Via della Greve 7-9, tel. 2048713. **Poggio Gaio**, Via San Michele a Monteripaldi 4, tel. 2280348, fax 225327.

YOUTH HOSTELS: **Archi Rossi**, Via Faenza 94, tel. 290804, fax 2302601, newly opened in 1994, near the main station, approximately 80 beds. **Santa Monaca**, Via Santa Monaca 6, tel. 268338, fax 280185, privately run, fairly busy due to its central location, cooking facilities available. **Villa Camerata**, Viale A. Righi 2-4, tel. 601451, located quite far from the center on the outskirts of Florence, situated in a park, rooms with 10-20 beds – not ideal if you like night life, but in historical surroundings.

APARTMENT-SHARING CENTER: Via Orti Oricellari 10, tel. 287530, fax 295253 (Mon-Fri 10 am to 6 pm).

🏕 **Campeggio Michelangelo** (Campeggio Italiani e Stranieri), Viale Michelangelo 80, tel. 6811977, fax 689348, open all year. **Villa Camerata**, Viale A. Righi 2-4, tel. 601451 or 600315, fax 610300, open all year.

🍴 **Antico Ristoro di' Cambi**, Via S. Onofrio 1, tel. 217134, good simple home cooking, middle price range, closed Sunday. **La Baraonda**, Via Ghibellina 67r, tel. 2341171. Friendly trattoria, light typical Florentine cuisine, prices fair for quality offered. Closed Sunday and Monday lunchtime. **Burde**, Via Pistoiese, 6r, tel. 317206. One of the last traditional old trattorias of Tuscany. Excellent simple fare. Closed evenings and holidays. **La Carabaccia**, Via Palazzuolo 190, for less well-off gourmets, select fine main courses, exquisite wines. Closed Sunday and Monday lunchtime. **Cibreo**, Via dei Macci 118r, tel. 2341100. Typical Tuscan dishes, prices alright for the quality. Closed Sunday and Monday. **Dino**, Via Ghibellina 51r, tel. 241452. Closed Sunday evening and Monday. **Enoteca Pinchiorri**, Via Ghibellina 87, tel. 242777. One of the top Italian restaurants. The high prices reflect the quality offered. Closed Sunday, Monday and Wednesday lunchtime. **Le Fonticine**, Via Nazionale 79r, tel. 282106. Good, reasonably-priced cuisine, many home-made specialties. Closed Sunday and Monday. **Alle Murate**, Via Ghibellina 52r, tel. 240618. Dishes from various Italian regions. Closed Monday. **Pallottino**, Via Isola delle Stinche 1, tel. 289573, Tuscan cuisine, reasonable prices, closed Monday. **Ruggero**, Via Senese 89r, tel. 220542. Typical Florentine trattoria, good prices. Closed Tuesday and Wednesday. **Sabatini**, Via de Panzani 9, near central station, wickedly expensive gourmet shrine. **Alla Vecchia Bettola**, Viale Ariosto 32-34, tel. 224158, Tuscan cuisine, fairly expensive, closed Sunday and Monday.

A traditional Florentine specialty is the lampredotto. This is a sandwich roll served with strips of seasoned stewed tripe, which can also be ordered "bathed" (bagnato) in broth. Good places to sample this local treat are **Nerbone**, in the Mercato Centrale, and the small snack stands found on Piazza dei Cimatori and Piazza Ghiberti.

☕ **Antico Caffe Torino**, Viale Matteotti 2, tel. 588247. **Caffetteria Gilli**, Piazza della Repubblica 1r, tel. 213896. A "must" in Florence. **Chez Moi**, Via di Porta Rossa 15, tel. 27232, nightclub. **Genesi**, Piazza del Duomo 20, directly opposite the Cathedral, drinking establishment with bar, always full. **Moulin Rouge**, Via Baccio Bandinelli, tel. 208608, nightclub. **Paszkowski**, Piazza della Repubblica 6r, tel. 210236. Attractive street café, excellent ice cream. **Pozzo di Beatrice**, Piazza di Santa Trinita 5, tel. 270804, nightclub. **Rivoire**, Piazza d. Signoria 5r, tel. 214412. Chocolate specialities. **Roof Garden Baglioni**, Piazza dell'Unita d'Italia, tel. 23846, nightclub.

🍺 **Cotton Pub**, Via delle Terme 20, tel. 264140. **Kneype**, Viale Gramsci 1, tel. 2343890. **Spaziouno**, Via del Sole 10, pub with cinema, cheap drinks. In the cinema a one-time club fee is charged at the entrance.

🎵 **Jaragua**, near Piazzale Michelangelo, South American music, closed Mon. **Jazz Club**, Via Nuova de' Caccini 3, tel. 2479700. **Pongo**, Via Verdi 59, popular rock music café. **Red Garter**, Via dei Benci 33, rock music pub, live shows Thu, Fri, Sat. **Tenax**, Via Pratese 46, tel. 308160, fax 308160. **Villa Kasar**, Lungarno Colombo 23, tel. 676901, 676912, fax 332348.

🏛 MUSEUMS: **Uffizi Gallery**, Piazzale degli Uffizi, Tue-Sat 8:30 am to 10 pm (in winter to 6:50 pm), Sun 8:30 am to 8 pm (in winter to 1:50 pm), closed Mon. **Palazzo Pitti**: Galleria Palatina, Appartamenti Monumentali, Tue-Sat 8:30 am to 18:50 pm (in summer to 10 pm) Sun/hol 8:30 am to 1:50 pm (in summer to 8 pm); Museo delle Porcellane, Museo degli Argenti, every 2nd and 4th Mon and every 1st, 3rd and 5th Sun in the month 9 am to 2 pm. Galleria dell'Arte Moderna, Galleria del Costume, Tue-Sat 8 am to 1:50 pm, closed Mon. **Galleria dell' Accademia**, Via Ricasoli 60. Tue-

Sat 8:30 am to 10 pm (in winter to 6:50 pm), Sun 8:30 am to 8 pm (in winter to 1:50 pm), closed Mon. **Museo Nationale Bargello**, Via del Proconsolo 4, Tue-Sat 8:30 am to 1:50 pm, every 2nd and 4th Sun in the month 8:30 am to 1:50 pm, also open every 1st, 3rd and 5th Mon in the month. **Museo San Marco**, Piazza San Marco, same times as Museo Nationale Bargello. **Palazzo Davanzati (Museo dell'Antica Casa Fiorentina)**, Via Porta Rossa 13, Tue-Sat 9 am to 2 pm, Sat 9 am to 1 pm. **Museo Archeologico**, Via della Colonna 36, Tue-Sat 9 am to 2 pm, Sun 9 am to 1 pm, closed Mon. **Medici Chapels**, Piazza Madonna degli Aldobrandini, Tue-Sat 8:30 am to 4:50 pm, every 1st, 3rd and 5th Sun and 2nd and 4th Mon in the month 8:30 am to 1:50 pm. **Palazzo Vecchio and Quartieri Monumentali**, Piazza della Signoria. Mon/Tue/Wed/Fri 9 am to 7 pm, Thu 9 am to 2 pm, Sun/holi 8 am to 1 pm. **Palazzo Medici-Riccardi**, Via Cavour 1, Mon, Tue and Thu-Sat 9 am to 1 pm and 3 to 6 pm, Sun/hol 9 am-1 pm. **Museo dell'Opera del Duomo** (Cathedral Museum), Piazza Duomo 9, Mon-Sat 9 am to 7 pm, Feb-Oct also Sun 9 am to 2 pm. **Museo dell'Opera di S. Croce**, Piazza S. Croce 16. March-Oct 10 am to 12:30 pm and 2:30 to 6:30 pm, Nov-Feb Thu-Tue 10 am to 12:30 pm and 3 to 5 pm. **Museo di Storia della Scienza**, Piazza dei Giudici 1, Mon-Sat 9:30 am to 1 pm, Mon, Wed, Fri also 2 to 5 pm. **Museo Marino Marini**, Piazza S. Pancrazio, Mon and Wed-Sat 10 am to 5 pm, Sun 10 am to 1 pm, Thu in summer to 11 pm, closed in August. **Museo Stibber**, Via Stibbert 26, Mon-Wed and Fri 10 am to1 pm and 3 to 6 pm, Sat-Sun 10 am to 6 pm. Guided tours every half hour. **Pinacoteca della Certosa**, Certosa del Galluzzo, Tue-Sun 10 am to 1 pm and 3 to 6 pm (in winter to 5 pm). **Museo S. Ferragamo**, Designer shoe collection of the Hollywood "dream shoe" maker Ferragamo, Via dei Tornabuoni 2, Mon-Fri 9 am to 1 pm and 2 to 6 pm. *CHURCHES:* Most churches are open daily 8 am to noon and 4 to 6 pm. The **Cathedral** can be seen Mon-Sat 10 am to 5 pm, and Sun 1 to 5 pm. **Tours of the dome** 8:30 am to 6:20 pm, Sat 8:30 am to 5 pm (1st Sat in the month 8:30 am to 3:20 pm), closed Sun/hol. The **Baptistery** is open Mon-Sat noon to 6:30 pm, Sun/hol 8:30 am to 1:30 pm. Ascent of the **Campanile**, daily 9 am to 6:50 pm (summer), 9 am to 4:20 pm (winter). *MEDICI VILLAS:* **Villa di Castello** and **Villa della Petraia**, Nov-Feb daily 9 am to 4:30 pm, March and Oct 9 am to 5:30 pm, April-May/Sept 9 am to 6:30 pm, June-Aug 9 am to 7:30 pm, closed 2nd and 3rd Mon of the month. **Cerreto Guidi**, daily 9 am to 6:30 pm, closed 2nd and 3rd Mon of the month. **Poggio a Caiano**, in winter 9 am to 3:30 pm, in summer 9 am to 5:30 pm, closed 2nd and 3rd Mon of the month.

OFFICE FOR MUSEUM RESERVATIONS: **Musei Statali Firenze**, tel. 294883.
GUIDED TOURS: **Guide Turistiche Della Toscana**, Via Calimala 2, tel./fax 2302283. **Centro Guide Turismo – Firenze e Provincia**, Via Ghibellina 110, tel. 288448, fax 288476. **Guide Turistiche Fiorentine**, Via Ugo Corsi 25, tel./fax 4220901.
➕ **ACI:** (Italian Automobile Club) tel. 116. **Pharmacies** (open all day): **Comunale**, in the central train station, tel. 289435. **Insegna del Moro**, at the Cathedral. **Arcispedale di S. M. Nuova**, Piazza S. M. Nuova 1, tel. 27581. **Careggi**, Viale Morgagni 85, tel. 4277111.
🗓 **June 24** (*Calcio in Costume*), festival of the patron saint San Giovanni (St. John), traditional football game on Piazza della Signoria in remembrance of the unsuccessful siege of the city in the 16th century by Charles V; procession in historical costumes. **Easter Sunday** (*Scoppio del Carro*), fireworks display at the Cathedral, in which Mass is celebrated while two oxen draw a wooden cart (*carro*) in front of the portal; a flame from the portal sets off fireworks on the cart.
🛍 **Via Tornabuoni:** Everything that money can buy in the way of elegant fashion can be found on this exclusive shopping street. **Ponte Vecchio:** On this historic bridge over the Arno there is one tiny jewelry shop after another. **Mercato Cascine:** Every Tuesday morning there is a weekly market on the banks of the Arno (near the Ponte della Vittoria), you can find everything from cooking pots to chandeliers, and if you're good at bargaining, you can get them at low prices. **Straw Market**: Via Calimala, near the Piazza della Repubblica, typical goods for tourists: hats, handbags, leather goods, in past times more valuable goods were traded in this historical loggia, e.g., gold and silk .
🚓 *SAFETY:* Florence is a paradise for pickpockets who involve you in a harmless conversation while relieving you of your valuables! You should not even trust wide-eyed children: gangs of children practice a variety of clever methods of stealing. Use attended parking lots where possible. Don't leave valuables visible inside the car; it's best empty the glove compartment and leave it open. Should you lose something or be robbed, here are the most useful addresses: **Railway Police**: Tel. 212296. **Theft** (cars, property): Tel. 49771. **Fire Dep't**: 241841 or 115. **Lost and Found**: Via Circondaria 19 (9 am to noon), tel. 3283942. **Consulates**: US, Lungarno Vespucci 38, tel. 2398276; UK, Lungarno Corsini 2, tel. 284133/212594. **Ambulance**: Tel. 212222 (Misericordia), tel. 215555 (Fratellanza Militare), tel. 475411 (Doctors' Association), tel. 283394, 244444, 4976 (coronary illnesses), tel. 1118394 (24-hour ambulance). **Emergencies**: Tel. 113 or 318000. **Police** (Carabinieri): Tel. 112. **Traffic Police**: Tel. 32831 or 577777.

Around Florence

*FIESOLE

One of the most popular excursions for visitors to Florence has always been *Fiesole ❷, to the north of the city. As the Roman settlement *Faesulae*, it once overshadowed Florence on account of its favorable location high above the Arno and Mugnone valleys. Even before Roman times it was one of the 12 cities of the Etruscan League – remains of the city walls near the Roman amphitheater date from this period. Under the Romans, the city also boasted, in addition to this theater, a forum, a capitol, temples and baths. Fiesole was the center of the region, wealthy and powerful. The era of the great migrations came and went without leaving any major traces. But then, in 1125, Fiesole was conquered and destroyed by its strengthened rival Florence, and it never managed to recover fully from this blow.

After the 15th century, wealthy Florentine families, notably the Medici, started having summer residences built on the hills of Fiesole. These villas are situated amid beautiful surroundings on a steep, terraced slope just under the town, and command a spectacular view of Florence and the Arno Valley. If you follow a winding road, the *Via Vecchia Fiesolana*, it will take you up to the church and monastery of the little village of **San Domenico**, where the painter monk Fra Angelico was a novice before he moved to San Marco in Florence. The Altar of the Madonna in the church, in the first chapel on your left, is his work.

Not far from San Domenico is the **Badia Fiesolana ❸**, which was the cathedral church of Fiesole until the 11th century, after which its monastery was turned over to the Benedictines. During the Renaissance, the abbey was enlarged and rebuilt. In the façade of the church,

Left: Fiesole's steep streets will keep you in shape.

which was never quite completed, you can still see the light and dark stones of the old Romanesque façade. The interior is appointed in the style of Brunelleschi. To the right of the church is the entrance to the former convent.

Between the Badia and Fiesole's city center is the **Villa Medici** – also referred to as *Belcanto* or *Il Palagio di Fiesole*. This villa was built by Michelozzo for Cosimo the Elder between 1458 and 1461. It was here that Lorenzo the Magnificent entertained his literary friends, such as Poliziano, Pico della Mirandola and Landino. Today, the villa is privately owned and not open to the public.

The center of Fiesole is the **Piazza Mino da Fiesole ❶**, located on the site of the old Roman forum. To the north of the piazza lies the Romanesque Cathedral, **San Romolo ❷**, with its high crenellated campanile. A few steps further on is the entrance to the **Roman Theater ❸** and the archeological excavation site. The theater, which had a seating capacity of 3,000, dates back to the first century B.C.,

as do the remains of bathing facilities and those of a temple, which were discovered in a lower level. The north boundary of the excavation site is formed by the remnants of an Etruscan wall. Every year, the *Estate Fiesolana* festival stages theater performances and concerts in the Roman theater.

The **Museo Civico**, a building that resembles a temple, is immediately to the right of the entrance to the theater. Exhibited here are finds from the days of the Etruscans and Romans, as well as medieval artifacts. A little further on is the small but interesting **Museo Bandini ❹**, which displays Florentine paintings from the 13th to 15th centuries as well as Della Robbia terra cottas and wood carvings.

The lovely 14th-century Town Hall on the east side of the square is quite charming, and is adorned with numerous coats of arms. On the other side, adjacent to the

Above: Illustration for Boccaccio's Decameron (Francesco di Stefano, 15th century). Right: La Petraia – the Medici summer palace.

11th-century Bishop's Palace, the steep Via di San Francesco leads up to the **Franciscan Monastery ❺**. You can enjoy a beautiful view of Florence from the square in front of the monastery.

From Fiesole you reach **Poggio Gherardo ❹** by way of Maiano. In 1348, Boccaccio and 10 young Florentine aristocrats are supposed to have retreated to the **Villa di Poggio Gherardo** in the face of an outbreak of the plague in Florence. To pass the time, they exchanged ribald stories, which became the ostensible basis for Boccaccio's famous collection of novellas, the *Decameron*.

Continuing on, you'll come to **Ponte a Mensola** and the church of **San Martino**, which contains a triptych by Taddeo Gaddi. Nearby is the **Villa I Tatti**, which today houses Harvard University's Center for Renaissance History, as well as a valuable art collection. The road leads on toward Settignano by way of Coverciano. Just past Coverciano come the villas of **Porziuncola** and **Capponcina**, where Eleanora Duse and her lover Gabriele d'Annunzio lived at the beginning of the 20th century.

Settignano ❺ was the home town of such famous sculptors as Desiderio, the Rossellinos and Bartolomeo Ammannati. Not far off, near Terenzano, is one of the most beautiful Renaissance villas in Italy, the **Villa Gamberaia**. Heavily damaged during the Second World War, it was restored according to the original plans. It is principally notable for its magnificent park, which contains statues, fountains and waterworks. You might be able to visit this park if you contact the owners (tel. 055-697205).

THE MEDICI VILLAS

Some of the most famous villas built by the Medicis are on the northern outskirts of Florence. On the road that leads up to the slopes of Monte Morello and the mountains of Calvana, for example, you

will find the **Villa Medicea di Careggi**. Today, this is part of the huge hospital complex of the Florence Medical School. The villa, renovated by Michelozzo for Cosimo the Elder, is supposed to have been the Medici's favorite villa. It was here that Cosimo founded the Platonic Academy during the 15th century, which became a meeting place for celebrated writers, philosophers and artists.

Within a radius of a few miles there are three other famous villas. First, there's the **Villa Corsini** with its Baroque façade. To the left of this, the Via della Petraia leads to the **Villa Medicea della Petraia**, a former palace of the Brunelleschi family which was purchased by the Medicis in 1530. Ferdinand I then had the building magnificently redesigned and renovated by Buontalenti.

The gardens were laid out by Niccolò Pericolo, known as Tribolo, who also created the elegant fountains of Venere-Fiorenza with a statue by Giambologna. The terraces of the hanging gardens command a beautiful view of the city.

From Villa Corsini, continue along the Via di Castelloto to the **Villa Medicea di Castello**. In the 14th century, a fortified castle stood upon this spot. Lorenzo and Giovanni di Pierfrancesco de' Medici acquired the estate in 1477, and Cosimo I had it turned into an exquisite Renaissance villa. Here, too, it was Tribolo who was responsible for the layout of the beautiful park and for the fountain, which depicts Hercules doing battle with the giant Antaeus.

The renowned *Grotta degli Animali* (Grotto of the Animals) at the end of the central path was also designed by Tribolo, and fitted out with animal representations in different colors of marble by Ammannati and others (today, the bronze birds created by Giambologna can be seen in the Bargello Museum).

Since 1974, the **Villa di Castello** has been the headquarters of the *Accademia della Crusca*, the Italian language academy founded in 1583, which has been concerned with maintaining the purity of the Italian language ever since.

EXCURSION TO THE MUGELLO AND THE SIEVE VALLEY

If you want to see a part of Tuscany that's not overrun by tourists, take a trip into the Mugello and the Sieve Valley, the area east of the Bologna-Florence expressway. For this trip, start out on the old road that leads over the Apennines toward Bologna, the SS 65, running through a landscape dotted with villas and gardens. The first town you'll come to is **Pratolino ❻**, a spot famous for its **Villa Demidoff** (as it is called today), which Grand Duke Francesco de' Medici had built by Buontalenti for his mistress (later his wife), Bianca Cappello, in the 16th century. The villa is surrounded by a wonderful park with numerous fountains, grottoes and statues, including the huge Apennine Statue by Giambologna. In summer the park is open to the public all day from Thursday to Sunday.

Continue on to **San Piero a Sieve ❼** in the Sieve Valley, which is dominated by the impressive Medici fortress of San Martino. Immediately after San Piero a Sieve comes the fortress-like edifice of the **Villa Medicea di Cafaggiolo**, which was built by Michelozzo for Cosimo I as a summer residence. Lorenzo the Magnificent used it later as a hunting lodge.

A few kilometers further on, a small road turns off to the right and leads to the Franciscan monastery of ***Bosco ai Frati ❽**, which Cosimo's architect Michelozzo, who also designed the nearby **Castello di Trebbio**, practically rebuilt from scratch. A precious wooden crucifixion carved by Donatello is on display in the diminutive Museo d'Arte Sacra in the chapter-room of the monastery.

The route continues past Barberino di Mugello and leads over the Futa Pass (903 meters), where one of the largest cemeteries for German soldiers in Italy was laid out between 1962 and 1965. Eight kilometers further on, the road intersects with the SS 503, which takes us back to San Piero a Sieve by way of Firenzuola and the Giogo di Scarperia.

Firenzuola ❾, or Little Florence, a spa town and tourist center 422 meters above sea level, was founded by the Florentines during the 12th century so that they could control the road to Bologna. During World War II, it was almost completely destroyed, but later was rebuilt according to the original rectangular ground plan.

Scarperia ❿ is one of the more important towns in the Mugello. The medieval center of the town, which was founded by the Republic of Florence during the 12th century to control the pass road through the Apennines, is still very well preserved. The façade of the Palazzo Pretorio with its high, turreted campanile, is

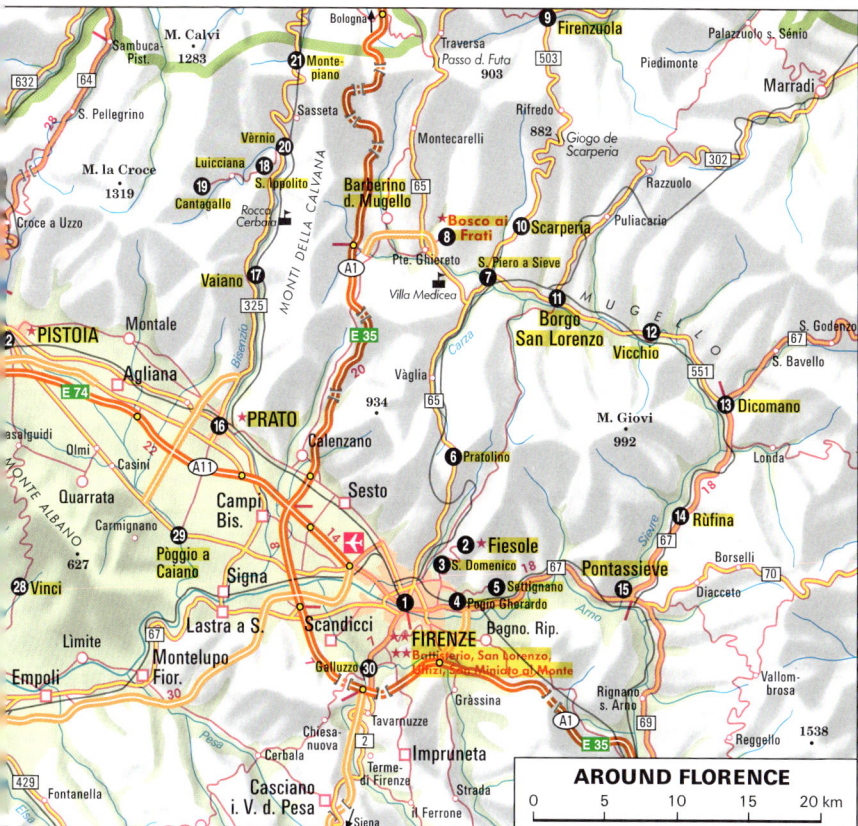

Map labels:

Bologna | Firenzuola ⑨ | Palazzuolo s. Sénio | Piedimonte | Marradi
M. Calvi 1283 | Traversa | Passo d. Futa 903 | Rifredo 882 | Giogo de Scarperia | Razzuolo | 302 | Puliacario
Sambuca Pist. | 632 | 64 | S. Pellegrino | Montepiano ㉑ | Sasseta | Montecarelli | 503
M. la Croce 1319 | Vèrnio ⑳ | Luicciana | S. Ippolito ⑱ | Cantagallo ⑲ | Rocca Cerbaia | Barberino d. Mugello 65 | Bosco ai Frati ⑧ | Pte. Ghieroto | S. Piero a Sieve ⑦ | Scarperia ⑩ | S. Godenzo | 67 | S. Bavello
Croce a Uzzo | MONTI DELLA CALVANA | Vaiano ⑰ | 325 | A1 | Villa Medicea | Borgo San Lorenzo ⑪ | Vicchio ⑫ | 551 | Londa | Dicomano ⑬
PISTOIA | Montale | E 35 | Carza | Vàglia | M. Giovi 992 | Diacceto
Agliana | E 74 | 934 | 65 | Prafolino ⑥ | Rùfina ⑭ | Borselli | 70
asalguidi | Olmi | Casini | PRATO | Calenzano | Sesto | Fiesole ② | S. Domenico ③ | Pontassieve | 67
MONTE ALBANO | Quarrata | Campi Bis. | Settignano ⑤ | Poggio Gherardo ④ | ⑮ | Vallombrosa
Carmignano | Pòggio a Caiano 627 | Signa | Scandicci | FIRENZE ① | Bagno. Rip. | Rignano s. Arno | 1538
Vinci ㉘ | Lìmite | Lastra a S. | Galluzzo ㉚ | Battistero, San Lorenzo, Uffizi, San Miniato al Monte | A1 | 69 | Reggello
Montelupo Fior. | Tavarnuzze | Gràssina | E 35
Empoli | Chiesa-nuova | 2 | Impruneta | Rignano
429 | Fontanella | Cerbala | Terme di Firenze | Casciano i. V. d. Pesa | il Ferrone | Strada | Siena

AROUND FLORENCE

0 — 5 — 10 — 15 — 20 km

---

adorned with coats-of-arms of stone and ceramic. There is a tabernacle ascribed to Andrea della Robbia contained in the oratory of the Madonna di Piazza, where the curates once swore their oath of allegiance upon taking office.

The 5.3-kilometer Mugello race track is on the outskirts of Scarperia. It was built by Florence's Automobile Club in 1974 and was recently modernized so that Formula 1 races can be held here.

Borgo San Lorenzo ⑪, Mugello's capital, is a center of agriculture and industry, particularly brick making and artistic ceramics. The church of San Lorenzo dates back to the 13th century; its hexagonal campanile, built entirely of brick, is from the same period. The façade was severely damaged during an earthquake in 1919, but it was rebuilt, using the old material, during the 1920s.

From Borgo San Lorenzo, continue following the Sieve Valley downstream for about seven kilometers to the village of **Vicchio** ⑫, the birthplace of the Dominican monk and painter Fra Angelico (ca. 1387-1455). On the square named after the painter Giotto (who was born in the neighboring village of Vespignano) stands the Palazzo Pretorio, which houses the Museo Beato Angelico, displaying sacred art from the Mugello.

The town of **Dicomano** ⑬, at the intersection with the SS 67, the *Tosco Romagnola*, was already established in the days of the Romans, and has always

served as a transportation hub, and therefore as a trade center, of the Sieve Valley. It is for this reason that the little city was spared by the Florentines when they conquered all of the castles in the area during the 14th century. Dicomano suffered severe damage as the result of a number of earthquakes, the most recent of which was in 1919. It was rebuilt during the 1940s, but unfortunately hardly anything is left of the old town.

Rufina ⑭, which is renowned for its good wine, lies on the road to Pontassieve. There's a wine museum located in the cellars of the 16th-century Villa di Poggio Reale. To arrange visits and for general information, contact tel. 055-8369848.

From **Pontassieve** ⑮, an old trade center at the confluence of the Sieve and Arno rivers, it is an 18-kilometer drive back to Florence.

Above: Michelozzo's famous exterior pulpit (1434-1438) on the Cathedral in Prato with its marvelous reliefs by Donatello.

*PRATO

*Prato ⑯ lies on the plain between Florence and Pistoia at the beginning of the Bisenzo Valley. Excavations have shown that there were already settlements here during the early Stone Age. Later, Prato came under Roman rule and subsequently developed into a larger settlement during the Lombardian period. In the 12th century it became a free imperial city. This ushered in a burst of economic development, which wasn't slowed down even when the city came under the sway of the ubiquitous Florentines in 1350.

Since the Middle Ages, Prato has had the weaving and cloth industry to thank for its exceptional prosperity. The development of a modern textile industry since the 19th century has made this city – which after World War II even started recycling rags into cheap new garments – into a kind of "Manchester of Tuscany." In the city's countless mills and factories, all manner of wool and woollens are processed into finished products each and every day. Today, Prato, with its approximately 170,000 inhabitants, is one of the wealthiest cities in Italy.

Some 600 years ago, a local merchant, Francesco di Marco Datini, invented not only the bank draft as a means of making payments without cash, but also double-entry bookkeeping. And yet, for all their love of cash and commerce, the business-minded Pratese have by no means overlooked art and culture. The old center of the city boasts a wealth of old buildings, and even modern Prato has managed to maintain a feeling for the arts.

The center of the hexagonal downtown area, encompassed by a 14th-century city wall, is the Piazza Communale, with its medieval Town Hall and the **Palazzo Pretorio** ❶, which houses the valuable art collection of the municipal museum.

From here, Via Mazzoni leads to the Cathedral square and the ***Cattedrale di Santo Stefano** ❷, an excellent example of Romanesque-Gothic architecture. From outside, the Cathedral displays a typically Tuscan exterior with stripes of pale white and green serpentine marble. Over the main portal is a relief by Andrea della Robbia, while on the right side of the façade projects the famous **outdoor pulpit** built by Michelozzo in 1434-1438, which Donatello furnished with magnificent bas-reliefs of dancing children (the originals can be seen in the Cathedral Museum, located in the Bishop's Palace). From this pulpit, the *Pergamo del Sacro Cingolo* (Pulpit of the Holy Girdle), the faithful are given a chance several times a year to glimpse a belt said to have belonged to the Virgin Mary, which was brought to Prato in 1141 by a local crusader when he returned home.

The interior of the Cathedral consists of a Romanesque nave, flanked by massive columns of green serpentine marble, and a Gothic transept. The marble pulpit is by Mino da Fiesole and Rossellino, while the main altar bears a wooden crucifix by Ferdinando Tacca. Most impressive, however, are the choir frescoes by Fra Filippo Lippi, a masterpiece of the early Renaissance. Particularly successful is the *Dance of Salome* (on the right), one of the series of frescoes illustrating scenes from the life of John the Baptist. Legend has it that the painter monk, who was not at all indifferent to the pleasures of the flesh, depicted in Salome his mistress, the nun Lucrezia Buti, who bore him two children. Their son, Filippino, later followed in his father's footsteps and became a famous artist.

Another church worth seeing is **Santa Maria delle Carceri** ❸ on the Via Cairoli, a beautiful domed building that was erected by Sangallo between 1485 and 1492. The church stands on the remains of an old prison (*carceri*), on the wall of which was painted an image of Mary said to have miraculous properties. The marble exterior of the church was never completed, but the building's archi-

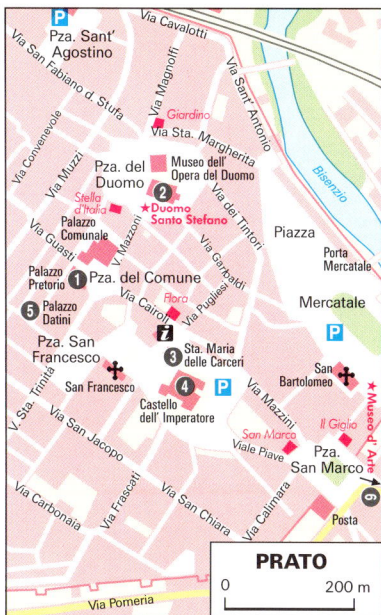

tectural proportions are magnificent. The interior contains a beautiful majolica frieze by Andrea della Robbia.

Across from the church is the **Castello dell'Imperatore** ❹, the Emperor's Fortress, which Frederick II had built in the 13th century on top of the old castle of the counts of Alberti. The mighty walls and towers with their swallow-tail merlons are reminiscent of the Hohenstaufen castles in Apulia and Sicily. Because of Frederick's death in 1250, the courtyard was never completed; nowadays it is used as an open-air stage for plays and concerts.

Not far from here is the **Palazzo Datini** ❺ on the Via Rinaldesca, which Datini, the wealthy banker and merchant mentioned above, had built for himself. In 1870, 460 years after Datini's death, numerous accounts ledgers, insurance policies, partnership contracts and business letters were discovered in a hiding place beneath the staircase. Today, this valuable documentary material is kept in the archives of the palace.

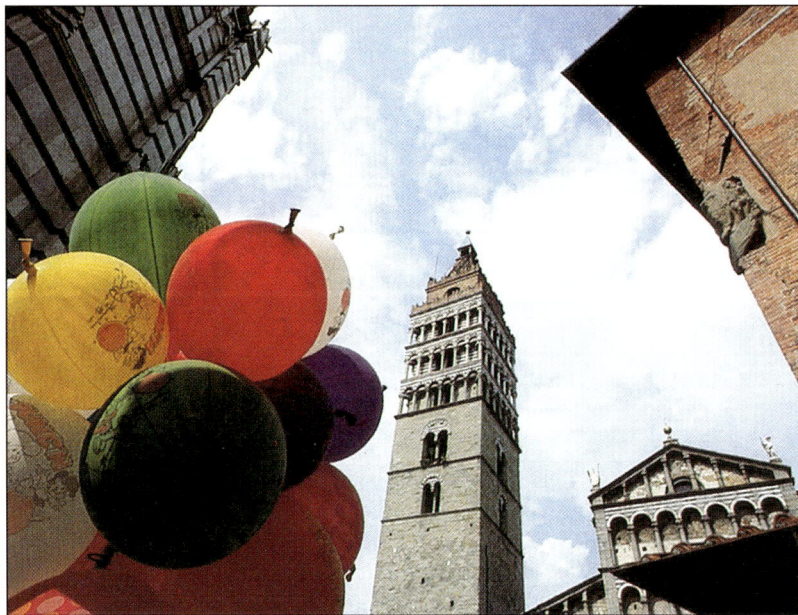

Examples of modern art in Prato can be found on the Piazza San Marco on the eastern edge of the old town center, where an impressive white marble sculpture by Henry Moore stands in the middle of a green lawn. If you depart from the Piazza San Marco and head south, you will pass through the modern sections of the city (the Institute for Textile Technology and the Textile Museum, founded in 1886, are both located on the Viale della Repubblica) before coming to the ***Museo d'Arte Contemporanea Luigi Pecci** ➏ (1988), which houses not only a museum of modern art, but a research center and the Center for Information and Documentation (CID) as well.

If you leave the old city center in a northerly direction by way of the Piazza Mercatale, you'll come to a bridge spanning the Bisenzio, which could be your point of departure for an excursion into the countryside around Prato.

Above: The 67-meter-high campanile of the Cathedral of Pistoia.

The Bisenzio Valley

From Prato, the highway SS 325 heads northward to Bologna, parallel to the expressway and railway tracks. It follows the **Bisenzio Valley** to the border of Tuscany and Emilia, between the karst slopes of the Monti della Calvana and the wooded ridge of the Apennines. Ever since the age of industrialization, the valley has always been densely settled, as the Bisenzio River supplied the countless textile factories, mills, paper factories and copper plants with water.

In a green hollow full of olive groves lies **Vaiano** ➐, center of the modern textile industry. During the Middle Ages, this town was an important military outpost for Prato.

The 11th century saw construction of the Badia di San Salvatore, of which the church, with an impressive campanile dating back to the 13th century, remains today. The triple-naved interior of the church is reminiscent of Prato's Cathedral. The sacristy, with wooden inlays from the 18th century, is of interest, as is the cloister (14th century) with its colonnaded portico and loggia.

Further north, the ruins of **Rocca Cerbaia**, which was a castle of the Alberti family in the 12th century, perch on a steep cliff. To get there, you have to walk up a small path which begins just past the little medieval bridge and ends at Montecuccoli, a village on the ridge of the Calvana, 633 meters high.

From Mercatale di Vernio, at the confluence of the Fiumenta and Bisenzio rivers, a steep road leads up to the health resort of **San Ippolito** ⑱ (415 meters), a town famous for its *carnevalino* (carnival and fair) on Ash Wednesday. Another road leads across the Bisenzio and through the lofty town of Lucciana to **Cantagallo** ⑲, where you can depart on a lovely hike up to the Pacini hut on the Pian della Rasa (1,001 meters).

After Mercatale, you come to the mouth of the 18-kilometer-long train tunnel that cuts through the Apennines and, once past this, you will arrive at **San Quirico di Vernio** ⑳ in the Fiumenta Valley, above which looms a fortress with remnants of an old castle. On the first Sunday in Lent, the traditional *Sagra della Polenta* is held here (the polenta is made using chestnut flour).

A steep climb takes you to one of the more easily traversable Apennine passes, which brings you over into Emilia Romagna and onto a sunny plateau where the pretty little health resort of **Montepiano** ㉑ is situated; like many mountain towns, this is also a good point of departure for a number of different hikes along well-marked trails.

★ PISTOIA

★Pistoia ㉒, like Prato, also stands in the cultural and political shadow of the more important cities of Florence, Lucca and Pisa. But it should not be neglected for this reason, as its old town center has a

number of important works of art that bear comparison with other, more renowned ones in Tuscany.

Pistoia goes back to the Roman era, when it was a fortified village on the Via Cassia. But it had its heyday during the 12th and 13th centuries, when it declared itself a free municipality. It was in this period that the buildings went up which still grace the historic part of the town center.

The best starting point for a walk through the Old Town – which is based on a rectangular ground plan and is still surrounded by the remains of a 14th-century city wall – is the picturesque **Piazza del Duomo** ❶, which is lined with a number of important buildings.

On the southeast side of the piazza rises the **★Domo San Zeno**, whose 67-meter-high campanile, the lower part of which resembles the tower of a fortress, is the trademark of the city. The Romanesque-Pisan church (12th/13th centuries) was built on the site of another church which dated from the 5th century. Its well-proportioned marble façade, with a

porch supported on slender columns, is decorated with a relief of the Madonna and majolica coffers by Andrea della Robbia. Among a number of notable artworks in the interior, the most famous object is the **Silver Altar of St. Jacob**, a masterpiece of Italian silver smithing which took almost 200 years to complete (from 1287 to 1456).

Next to the Cathedral, the medieval **Bishop's Palace** (Palazzo Vescovile) forms the south side of the square. Adjoining it is the octagonal **Baptistery**, built in the 14th century according to designs by Andrea Pisano. Beside this is the **Palazzo Pretorio** (14th century), with painted and sculpted armorial bearings and an attractive interior courtyard which serves as a courthouse today.

On the northeast side of the piazza and to the left of the Cathedral is the **Palazzo Comunale**, a massive sandstone building

Above: The "Seven Works of Mercy" on the majolica frieze of the Ospedale del Ceppo. Right: Pulpit in Sant'Andrea by Pisano.

which was begun during the 13th century and finally, after many interruptions, completed in the 14th century. A 17th-century wing joins it to the Cathedral. On the ground floor, the façade is divided into five loggias, while arched window openings create the division in the three upper stories. Over this, the façade sports the Medici coat-of-arms and the papal keys in honor of the Medici Popes, Leo X and Clement VII. Next to the central window, you can make out a head carved in black marble; no one is quite sure as to the significance of this image. The palace houses the **Museo Civico**, which has an attractive painting collection.

If you leave the Piazza del Duomo and head northeast, the Via Pacini will take you to the **Ospedale del Ceppo** ❷, named for the hollow tree stump (*ceppo*) where alms were once collected. Built in the 13th or 14th century, the hospital, which is still in use today, was adorned with a beautiful portico in the 16th century. The façade sports a magnificent majolica frieze from the school of Della

Robbia depicting the Seven Works of Mercy.

The church of *Sant'Andrea* ❸, architecturally an interesting building in the Pisan style, contains a special treasure: the **Pulpit by Giovanni Pisano**, which was built between 1298 and 1301, or, in other words, before his pulpit in the Cathedral of Pisa. The relief panels show scenes from the life of Christ; the dramatic representation of the Massacre of the Innocents is particularly impressive.

Another architectural masterpiece is the church of **San Giovanni Fuorcivitas** ❹ on the Via Cavour, south of the Piazza del Duomo. A particularly notable feature of this church is its outer side wall, which is beautifully decorated with stripes of light and dark marble and geometrical patterns. Over the entrance is a terra-cotta relief by Gruamonte from Como, while the church's interior contains a holy-water font by Giovanni Pisano and a terra-cotta relief of the *Visitation*, which is ascribed to either Luca or Andrea della Robbia.

Things are more modern in the **Pallazo Tau** on Via Garibaldi, which is devoted to modern art. Displayed here is a collection of sculptures and drawings by Marino Marini, who was born in Pistoia.

Ice Machines and Snow Cannons

Pistoia's convenient location between Florence, Pisa and Lucca is not the only reason one might want to choose to stay longer in this area. Another enticement is the beautiful countryside behind Pistoia, ideal for long excursions, by foot or on horseback. An attractive wooded landscape, medieval villages, old traditions and festivals are all reasons to get to know the Pistoian Apennines and their nature parks. One specialty of the region are the so-called *ghiaccai*, devices which in the 19th and early 20th centuries were used to keep ice which had been "mined" in the mountains cool and to transport it

down to the cities on the plain. Until the invention of artificial ice, this was the sole source of income for many families in the Reno Valley. You can see a few of these devices displayed in Le Piastre, about 20 kilometers from Pistoia.

And Pistoia's back country isn't only popular during the summer. In winter, the ski area around **Abetone** becomes a paradise for all manner of winter sports (recently, snow cannons have made it possible to ski no matter what the snow conditions are).

Baths, Flowers and a Wooden Scamp

The renowned health resort of **Montecatini Terme** ㉓ is one of the most elegant thermal spas in Italy, and its waters were probably known and valued even in Antiquity. Since the late 18th century, palazzo-like edifices have been built over the 11 springs, which are said to be especially good for people suffering from liver disorders and rheumatism. With beautiful parks, large hotels, and tidy or-

Above: The healing waters of Montecatini.

ganization, this town is an ideal place for anyone looking for a way to combine the necessity of a "cure" with pleasant surroundings. It is not, however, so interesting for anyone looking for the "real Tuscany." The same holds true of nearby **Monsummano ㉔**, which offers natural steam baths in caves. The hot and healing steam from the bowels of the earth can be enjoyed in the natural Grotta Giusti or in the artificial Grotta Parlanti.

There are a number of different excursions which could enliven a "cure." Take the medieval villages of **Montecatini Alto** and **Monsummano Alto**; or Valdinievole in the north, with its old mountain villages and villas; or the neighboring town of **Pescia ㉕**, with its famous flower market.

A few kilometers past Pescia is the village of **Collodi ㉖**, a name which Carlo Lorenzini, the author of *Pinocchio*, adopted as a *nom de plume*. In addition to

Pinocchio Park, which boasts life-sized wooden figures from the tales of the long-nosed puppet, this medieval village spread along the slope of a hill includes the **Villa Garzoni**, which has truly beautiful gardens.

LOWER ARNO VALLEY AND MONTALBANO

The drive from Monsummano on the SS 436 leads through the marshy areas of Fucecchio, with its unusual flora and fauna, to the Arno Valley, where the town of **San Miniato ㉗** extends along a mountain ridge on the south side. Because of its strategic location high above the valleys of the Arno, the Elsa and the Egola, the town was of military significance even during the Roman era. During the reign of the German emperor Otto I it became the seat of the imperial palatinate in Tuscany. Today, San Miniato is a quiet little town that only becomes lively in autumn, when it hosts a popular truffle festival (the third Saturday in October). And in November, a market for white truffles is held here every weekend.

One noteworthy sight is the **tower**, the last remnant of a castle that Frederick II had built high above San Miniato. Below this, on the tree-shaded Prato del Duomo, is the 13th-century **Cathedral** with its proud campanile.

Between San Miniato and Empoli, on the highway leading from Livorno to Florence, a small road turns off to the left, which takes you across the Montalbano ridge to Pistoia. This winding, yet extremely lovely scenic road passes through dense olive groves on its way to **Vinci ㉘**, birthplace of none other than Leonardo. There's a museum devoted to him in the old castle, while the house where he is supposed to have been born is actually a bit outside of town near Achiano, almost hidden behind olive trees and cypresses. Here, too, you can see exhibits and reproductions of some of his works.

FIESOLE (☎ 055)

ℹ️ **Tourist Information Office**, Piazza Mino 36, tel. 598720, fax 598822.

🛏️ ⊝⊝⊝ **Villa San Michele**, Via Doccia 4, tel. 59451, fax 598734. **Villa Aurora**, Piazza Mino 39, tel. 59100, fax 59587. ⊝⊝ **Villa Bonelli**, Via F. Poeti 1a, tel. 59513, fax 598942. **Bencistà**, Via B. da Maiano 4, tel./fax 59163. **Dino**, Via Faentina 329, tel. 548932. **Villa Fiesole**, Via Fra' Giovanni Angelico 35, tel. 597252, fax 599133. ⊝ **Villa Baccano**, Via Bosconi 4, tel./fax 59341. **Villa Sorriso**, Via Gramsci 21, tel./fax 59027.

AGRITURISMO (farmhouse holidays): **Azienda Agricola Terenzano**, Via della Rosa 15, tel. 6593021. **Fattoria di Poggiopiano**, Via dei Bassi 13, tel. 6593020.

🏕️ **Campeggio Panoramico**, Via Peramonda 1, tel. 599069, fax 59186.

❌ **Le Cave di Maiano**, Via delle Cave 16, tel. 59133. Traditional cuisine, country-style atmosphere. Prices are okay. Closed Monday lunchtime. **Pizzeria San Domenico**, San Domenico, tel. 59182. Closed Monday.

🏛️ *MUSEUMS:* **Civic Museum – Roman Theater**, Via Portigiani 1. Summer daily 9 am to 7 pm; winter daily 9 am to 5 pm. Closed Tuesdays. **Museo Bandini**, Via Duprè 1. Summer daily 10 am to 7 pm; winter 9:30 am to 4:30 pm, closed 1st Tues of the month. **Antiquarium Costantini**, Via Portigiani 1. Summer daily 9 am to 7 pm; winter 9:30 am to 5 pm, closed 1st Tues of the month. Valuable collection of antique ceramics.

SIGHTS: **Parco della Rimembranza** lookout point. **Church** and **Museum of San Francesco**, Via S. Francesco. Summer daily 10 am to noon and 3 to 6 pm; winter daily 10 am to noon and 3 to 5 pm. **Villa Gamberaia**, daily 8 am to sunset.

PRATO (☎ 0574)

ℹ️ **Tourist Information Office Prato,** Piazza Santa Maria delle Carceri 15, tel. 24112.

🚗 *CAR RENTAL:* **Avis**, Via della Repubblica 289, tel. 596619. **Hertz**, Viale Vittorio Veneto 57, tel. 21055. *TAXI:* **Radiotaxi**, tel. 5656. **Eurotaxi**, tel. 564061, 571676.

🛏️ ⊝⊝⊝ **Art Hotel Museo**, Viale della Repubblica 289, tel. 5787, fax 578880. **Palace**, Via Piero della Francesca 71, tel. 5671, fax 567267. **President**, Via A. Simintendi 20, tel. 30251-3. ⊝⊝ **Flora**, Via Cairoli 31, tel. 33521, fax 40289. **Giardino**, Via G. Magnolfi 2, tel. 606588, 26189. **San Marco**, Piazza S. Marco, tel. 21321-3. **Villa Santa Cristina**, Via Poggio Secco 58. tel. 595951, fax 572623. ⊝ **Stella d'Italia**, Piazza

Duomo 8, tel. 27910, fax 40289. **Il Giglio**, Piazza S. Marco 14, tel. 37049, fax 604351. **Roma**, Via G. Carradori 1, tel. 31777. **La Toscana**, Piazza G. Ciardi 3, tel. 28096.

❌ **Art Restaurant**, Viale della Repubblica 289, tel. 578888, closed Sun. **Barbarossa**, Via Tiziano 15, tel. 27331, 23371, closed Sun. **La Cucina di Paola**, Via Banchelli 16, tel. 24353, closed Mon. **Le Mura**, Via S. Antonio 24, tel. 24320, closed Mon. **Tonio**, Piazza Mercatale 161, tel. 21266, closed Sun and Mon. **Il Piraña**, Via Tobia Bertini, tel. 25746. Very modern design, high prices, but excellent fish dishes. Closed Sat lunchtime and Sunday. **Trattoria Lapo**, Piazza Mercatale 141, tel. 23745. Somewhat uninviting but with very folkloric character, closed Sun. **La Vecchia Cucina di Soldano**, Via Pomeria 23, tel. 34665, Trattoria, closed Sun.

🏛️ **Palazzo Datini**, Via Ser Lapo Mazzei, 9 am to noon and 3 to 6:30 pm, closed Sundays and holidays, free entry. **Museo d'Arte Contenporanea Luigi Pecci**, daily 10 am to 7 pm. Closed Tuesdays. **Medici Villa** in **Poggio a Caiano**, 8 km south of Prato. Summer daily 9 am to 5:30 pm; winter daily 9 am to 3:30 pm, closed 2nd and 3rd Monday of the month.

➕ **Ospedale Misericordia e Dolce**, Piazza dell' Ospedale, tel. 6011.

PISTOIA (☎ 0573)

ℹ️ **A.P.T. Pistoia**, Via Roma 1, Palazzo dei Vescovi, tel. 21622, fax 34327.

🛏️ ⊝⊝ **Leon Bianco**, Via Panciatichi 2, tel. 26675, fax 26704. **Milano**, Viale Pacinotti 10, tel. 975700, fax 32657. **Patria**, Via F. Crispi 6, tel. 25187, fax 368168. **Piccolo Ritz**, Via A. Vannucci 67, tel. 26775, fax 27798. **Hotel Le Rose**, Viale Adua 89, tel. 20785, fax 976161. **Signorino**, Il Signorino, Via Bolognese 207, tel. 475162 or 475070, fax 475162. **Il Convento**, Via S. Quirico 33, Loc. Ponte Nuovo, tel. 452651, fax 453578. ⊝ **Autisti**, Viale Pacinotti 89, tel. 21771. **Il Boschetto**, Viale Adua 467, tel. 401336. **Firenze**, Via Curtatone e Montanara 42, tel. 21660, fax 23141.

❌ **Leon Rosso**, Via Panciatichi, 4, tel. 29230. Closed Sun. **La Vela**, Piazza dell'Ortaggio 12, tel. 33658, good cuisine, low prices, closed Sun evening and Mon.

🏛️ **Museo Civico**, open Tue-Sat 9 am to 6 pm, Sun 9 am to 12:30. **Palazzo Tau**, Tue-Sat 9 am to 1 pm and 3 to 7 pm. **Gardens of the Villa Garzoni in Collodi**, Nov-March Mon-Fri 9 am to 1 pm and 2:30 pm to sunset, Sat-Sun 9 am to sunset; April-Oct 9 am to sunset. **Pinocchio Park**, daily 9 am to sunset. **Museo Vinciano** (in Vinci Castle), summer daily 9:30 am to 7 pm; winter until 6 pm.

Around Florence

59

FROM SIENA TO CHIANTI

SIENA

SAN GIMIGNANO

VOLTERRA

★★SIENA – CITY OF THE PALIO

Since time immemorial, the Sienese have been known for their collective pride: Dante described them as a "proud people" as early as the 14th century. And they have reason to be proud: **★★ Siena ❶** has preserved its medieval appearance in a marvelous fashion, keeping up its traditions and barring the damaging inroads of modernity from its city center, which was made a pedestrian zone in 1956. This all helps to keep Siena one of the most fascinating cities in Tuscany, despite the hordes of tourists continually streaming through. Wandering through the narrow streets between the old brick façades, you sense that you're in a living Italian city which, for all of its art treasures, has a vibrant, rather than museum-like, air.

Siena's residents have always set special store by the beauty of their city. And because of this, the city is truly a work of art in itself: it was built according to careful plan, following exact regulations and restrictions which had to be strictly upheld. In the 14th century, for example, the city government ruled that all of the windows on the Piazza del Campo had to correspond to those of the Town Hall; no one

Left: Parade of flag-wavers at the Palio in Siena.

was to be allowed to ruin the city's image by following his own whim. And this, like so many Sienese traditions, has been upheld to the present day.

Little is known of Siena's beginnings. Legend has it that Ascius and Senius, the sons of Remus, were forced to flee their uncle Romulus, Rome's founder, and subsequently founded this city on three hills in Etruria. But the story, which dates back to the Renaissance, is merely a charming fiction invented by the Sienese themselves; although it explains why you see the symbol of the Roman she-wolf throughout the city.

The city didn't become truly important until the Middle Ages, when, located on the old trade route of the Frankish Road, it developed into a center of finance and trade. Resources of silver in the surrounding hills helped Siena to attain wealth and power. In 1472, one of the first great banks, Monte dei Paschi, was founded – and it's still going strong.

In the 13th century, the Republic of Siena numbered some 20,000 inhabitants, which made it a major urban center for that period. It continued to flourish until the 16th century, although engaged in constant skirmishes and power struggles with its hated rival, Florence. In 1260, Florence was defeated in the Battle of Montaperti; but a mere nine years later

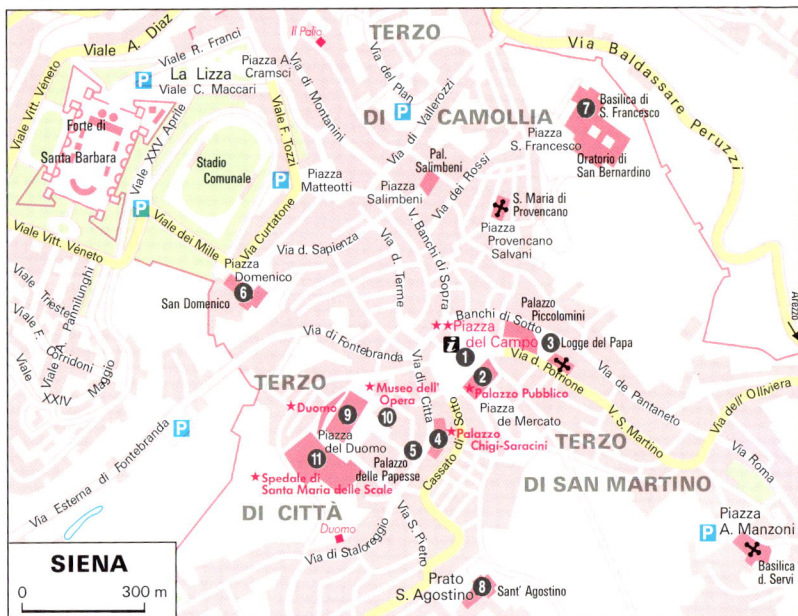

the Sienese were in turn beaten at Colle di Val d'Elsa by Florentine troops. Under the Guelph regime of the Council of Nine which followed (1292-1355), important artists were drawn to the city, including Duccio di Buonisegna, Simone Martini, Pietro and Ambrogio Lorenzetti, and the sculptor and architect Nicola and Giovanni Pisano. Their work helped shape the appearance of today's Siena and made it a true city of the arts.

Decline set in with the Black Death in 1348; Siena never fully recovered. For some 150 years, the city was shaken by inner unrest, which the efforts of Siena's great, and later canonized, heroes, St. Catherine and St. Bernard, or of Pope Pius II, a scion of the Sienese Piccolomini family, were able to dispel altogether. Finally, Emperor Charles V, an ally of Florence, stepped in, and in 1555 the city was incorporated into the Medici Duchy

Above: The shell-shaped Piazza del Campo in Siena is held to be one of the loveliest squares in the world.

of Tuscany. Although Siena has been forced into the secondary position of a provincial town ever since, you can still sense traces of its former enmity toward Florence, its one-time rival.

The city's silhouette is visible from afar, crowning the three hills over which Siena has spread in a roughly Y-shaped form, and dominated by the towers of the Town Hall and the mighty, black-and-white striped Cathedral. The narrow medieval streets wind crookedly between houses of reddish-brown brick (artists use a pigment of this shade called "sienna"), and lead uphill and down, so that it's hard to keep your sense of direction. At every corner in the Old Town, however, signposts are mounted so that you can always find your way back to the Campo or a number of the town's other major sights.

****Piazza del Campo**

The secular center of the city is a piazza which is one of the most beautiful in Italy, if not in the entire world: the

Piazza del Campo ❶. It lies like a great seashell in the hollow between the three hills of the town. Its red brick cobbles divide it into nine clear sections; arranged around this in a semicircle are the lovely, clearly-ordered palaces. In some of the façades, groups of three pointed-arched windows separated by little columns reflect the prescriptions of the medieval building codes. At the upper edge of the piazza, roughly in the middle, splashes the **Fonte Gaia (Spring of Joy). The fountain's original reliefs by Jacopo della Quercia are displayed in the Palazzo Pubblico.

The **Palazzo Pubblico**, or Town Hall, with its slightly crooked walls, forms the lower edge of the Campo. This gorgeous Gothic building, constructed between 1297 and 1310, perfectly reflects the pride and unbroken will to freedom that has always characterized the people of Siena. Today, the palace still serves as the headquarters of the city's administration. In front of the palace's left wing is the **Cappella di Piazza**, built in 1352 after

the Black Death. Above it, the Town Hall tower, 88 meters high (102 meters, if you count its lightning rod), thrusts, brick-red and travertine-white, into the deep blue Sienese sky.

This is the **Torre del Mangia**, named after a sexton whose name was Mangia-guadagni (Money Eater), it is the work of eight different architects. Lippo Memmi is supposed to have designed the broad travertine platform, which affords a marvelous view of the red rooftops of the city and the hilly countryside around. To the right of the Capella di Piazza, you pass a portrait bust of the money-hungry sexton as you enter the Cortile del Podestà, ornamented with coats-of-arms. From here, you can climb the 332 steps to the top of the tower – a laborious climb, but not to be missed, nonetheless.

Inside the ***Palazzo Pubblico ❷**, a tour of the upper floor (the ground floor belongs to the municipal administration, and is not open to the public) takes you through a series of marvelously-appointed rooms filled with some re-

markable works of art. The Sala del Mappamondo contains two famous frescoes: the *Maestà* (1315) by Simone Martini and *The Knight Guido Riccio da Fogliano Riding to the Siege of Montemassi* (1328), attributed to the same artist. This fresco is the first known large-scale landscape painting in European art. In the Sala della Pace you can see the famous allegorical frescoes by Ambrogio Lorenzetti, depicting Just and Unjust Government and the effects of both in the city and the country. These were executed between 1338 and 1340, under the regime of the Council of Nine, to which these marvelous images, which are also interesting depictions of daily life in the 14th century, are dedicated.

The Palazzo's other rooms contain countless other highlights of Sienese art; it would be impossible to list them all here. Take time yourself to stroll through

Above: Participating in the Palio is an honor for every Sienese. Right: The race itself is a test of endurance for horses and riders.

with open eyes and enjoy at your own pace the finer points of works by Sodoma, Taddeo di Bartolo, Jacopo della Quercia and Sano di Pietro – to name only a few.

The *Palio

When you leave the Palazzo Pubblico and come back out onto the broad Piazza del Campo – where you might see a few idlers loafing around, tired tourists sitting in the sun and resting their feet, or a couple of children splashing about in the fountain – you may have trouble imagining that, twice a year, thousands of people crowd onto this square and overrun it completely. Every year since the 17th century, July 2 and August 16 have seen the *Palio delle Contrade*, a horse race in honor of the Virgin Mary in which the city's 17 historic quarters compete for a trophy. The Palio, or victory trophy, is a flag bearing the image of the Virgin, which is designed anew every year by a different artist.

The Palio is the most fascinating festival in all of Tuscany. It plays an important part in the city's life throughout the year, and the few weeks leading up to it see the preparations for the great event rising to an ever-increasing pitch of intensity.

A Sienese citizen is born into a *contrada*, or city neighborhood, and he remains a member of it his whole life long. A marked self-confidence and interaction according to certain fixed rules are characteristic of the individual contradas, whose members are bound into a fixed social unit. The notably low crime rate in Siena may well be a result of the special sense of community that this system engenders.

Practice races begin in the days leading up to the festival, during which the members of the different contradas start to heat up the competition with mocking songs and insults. By the time the big day rolls around, the tension in the city is palpable everywhere. As the space is too small for all 17 contradas to run at once, 10 of them participate in each palio: the seven that

didn't take part in to the last race, as well as three that are chosen by lot. The horses, too, are chosen by lot; and the jockeys are professionals brought in from outside, who have to complete the breakneck race around the square bareback. Not surprisingly, there are quite often spectacular falls, and because of the hard, trampled-down sand surface, brought in especially for the race, these often result in bad injuries.

Before the race begins, the horses and riders are blessed in the church of whichever contrada they're riding for; the Archbishop of Siena then blesses the individual teams, riding by his palace in a blaze of colorful historic costumes; and the Madonna in whose honor all this takes place certainly extends a protecting hand to all and sundry.

After a number of practice runs and a historic, festival parade, the race begins; and it lasts hardly more than a minute. Even if you've got to sweat it out for a while on the Campo in the broiling noonday sun in order to secure a good view of

the colorful spectacle, the experience is truly worth the effort. Of course, you can always try to purchase one of the extremely expensive seats on the grandstand, in the windows or on one of the overcrowded balconies around the square; but these plum positions are usually sold out far in advance of the event itself. Those who want to avoid the hustle and bustle can watch the event live on television.

After the race, there's a rush of relief which finds expression in cries of joy, wild embraces, or even tears. The victorious contrada marches through the city in triumph and gives thanks to the Mother of God in the church of the Madonna di Provanzano. And then the celebrations begin in earnest: there's one festive dinner after another – even the victorious horse takes part and is given a place of honor. Unfortunately, though, all of this is only open to the Sienese.

Above: Alleyway in Siena. Right: The Duomo towers over the city's rooftops.

The Palaces

The gorgeous old palaces of Siena, testimony to the city's past wealth, are easily reached on foot. On the Banchi di Sotto, near the Campo, is the Renaissance **Palazzo Piccolomini**, built in 1469, probably according to plans by Rossellino. Since 1885, this building has housed the city archives, including certificates and documents designed and executed by famous Sienese artists.

Opposite the Palazzo is the entrance to the university, one of the oldest in Italy, which is documented as early as the year 1240. Today, it is housed in the former monastery of St. Vigilio, which dates from the 16th century. A little further on is the **Logge del Papa** ❸, which the Renaissance Pope Pius II commissioned from the architect Antonio Federighi for his family.

At the intersection of the Banchi di Sotto with the Banchi di Sopra and the Via del Città stands the three-arched **Loggia della Mercanzia**, a 15th-century

Renaissance building lightened up with Late-Gothic elements. The Banchi di Sopra leads to the Piazza Salimbeni, where you can see the Gothic palace of the same name. To the right and left of it stand the Renaissance palaces Spanocchi (built in 1470 according to designs by Giuliano da Maiano) and Tantucci (1548), respectively. Today, these three palaces house the venerable Bank of Monte dei Paschi.

In the Via di Città, you can see the slightly crooked façade and the lovely inner courtyard of the Gothic **Palazzo Chigi-Saracini** ❹, today the seat of the Accademia Musicale Chigiana, founded in 1923 by Count Guido Saracini. In summer, fine concerts are performed here. Inside, the palace houses a wonderful art gallery, but you can only visit it by applying for special permission.

Somewhat further on, at number 126, is another Piccolomini palace, known as the **Palazzo delle Papesse** ❺ because it was commissioned by the sister of Pope Pius II. Built in the style of the Florentine Re-naissance, it was constructed between 1460 and 1465.

Siena's Churches

Siena has produced a number of great saints over the years, including the patron saint of Italy, Catarina di Siena. There's a small sanctuary in her honor at Vicolo del Tiratoio 15, just a few steps away from the church of **San Domenico** ❻. This powerful Gothic brick building, begun in 1226, is still a Dominican church today. Inside the building, a reliquary contains the head of St. Catherine. The chapel dedicated to her also contains two note-worthy frescoes by Sodoma, depicting the Fainting and the Ecstasy of St. Catherine. Other art treasures include the ciborium on the main altar and two wonderful marble angels.

Like the Dominicans, the Franciscans and the Augustines built their churches and monasteries at the edge of the city, probably because it gave them more room to construct and expand their large build-

Vinci · Signa · Lastra · FIRENZE · Pontassieve · Diacceto Pèlago

436 · Cerreto · Limite · Scandicci · Bagno Rip. · Vallom-brosa

Fucecchio · Montelupo · Galluzza · Gràssina

Empoli · Chiesanuova · 67

S. Croce · Villanova · S. Andrea in Percussina · Impruneta · S. Polo i. Chianti · E 35 · Regello

Castelfranco · Arno · 2 · 2 · 222 · 1 · Incisa i.V.d'A. · 395

S. Miniato · Montespèrtoli · Strada · il Ferrone · Passo di Pecorai · Figline Vald. · Castel-Franco

la Serra · Cambiano · S. Casciano i. V. d. Pesa · 10 · Le Bolle · A1

Casastrada · Castello di Vichiomaggio · Uzzano · Pte. s Stolli · S. Giovanni Vald.

Castel-fiorentino · Lucardo · Verrazzano · 4 · Greve · M.S. Michele 892 · Terranova

429 · Certaldo · 12 · Tavarnelle V. di Pesa · Montefioralle · Sambuca · Panzano · 5 · San Leolino · Montevarchi

Pecciolo · Castelfalfi · 13 · Bagnano · 11 · Barberino V. d'E · Lucarelli · 6 · Volpaia · Bàdia a Coltibuono

il Castagno · Gambassi · 2 · Tùmulo di Monte Calvario · 7 · Radda in Ch. · Gaiole in Ch. · Castello di Meleto

Camporbiano · 624 · ★ S. Gimignano · 14 · Poggibonsi · 8 · Castellina in Chianti · 408

Colle di Val d'Elsa · 16 · 222 · Castello di Brolio · 540

★ Volterra · 15 · 68 · Monteriggioni · 17 · Quercegrosa · Pianella · Castelnuovo

CHIANTI AND SIENA
0 · 5 · 10 km

Càsole d'Elsa · 554 · 541 · M. Maggio 671 · S. Dalmàzio · ★★ SIENA · 18 · E 78 · 326

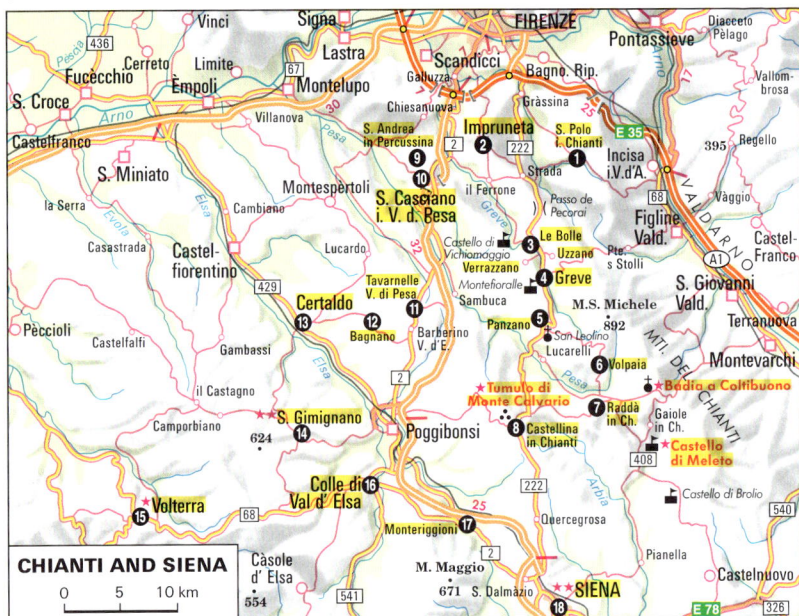

ing complexes. On the Piazza di San Francesco is the Gothic **Basilica di San Francesco** ❼, which contains wonderful frescoes by Ambrogio and Pietro Lorenzotti. Its crypt now houses the Law School library. Below the basilica, the upper story of the **Oratorio di San Bernardino** (a saint particularly beloved in Italy) shelters a number of paintings by Sodoma. The church of the Augustinian order, **Sant'Agostino** ❽ on Prato Sant' Agostino, also contains some marvelous works by Perugino, Matteo di Giovanni, Sodoma and Simone Martini.

The *Duomo

Siena's most famous church is at the center of the city, only a few paces from the Campo. The *Duomo ❾, or Cathedral, took some 200 years to build, and the mighty edifice you see today is only a portion of the building the ambitious

Right: Duccio di Buoninsegna's famous "Maestà" in the Cathedral Museum in Siena.

Sienese originally had in mind. It was, in fact, to be merely the transept of a huge new cathedral; but all that was actually realized of this mammoth edifice were the walls that you see to the right of the present Duomo. The devastating plague of 1348, high costs and political developments led to the abandoning of construction. What remains is a masterpiece of Italian Gothic, and certainly impressive enough in its own right.

Giovanni Pisano was the artist responsible for the Duomo's ornate signature green-and-white striped façade (1284-1296). The originals of his monumental statues and busts are today displayed in the Cathedral Museum. The central bronze portal is the work of the contemporary artist Enrico Manfrini from 1958. The mosaics at the top of the façade were completed in the late 18th century. On the right side of the building is the campanile, or bell tower, which is also executed in the same colors of contrasting marble.

Inside, the church with its three naves is veiled in a mystical twilight, with

echoes of a mosque in the 26 dichromatic columns, the blue ceiling with its gold stars, and the multicolored walls. The ornate floor, which occupied 40 artists for two centuries, is executed in a number of different techniques, from mosaic through sgraffito to marble inlay. The most valuable sections are protected by a wooden floor, and are unveiled only between August 15 and September 15. Looking down from a molding over the columns are the busts of Christ and 172 Popes, and, underneath them, 36 emperors from the 15th and 16th centuries. The stoup by the main entrance is the work of Antonio Federighi.

The Duomo's most important work of art, however, is the famous octagonal marble pulpit by Nicola Pisano and his son Giovanni (with some collaboration from other artists such as Arnolfo di Cambio and Donato). A coin automat operates the light, providing 60 seconds of illumination on the masterfully executed reliefs of biblical scenes. The expressive sculpted figures are full of life, their faces carved with individuality – you can see their descendants on the streets of modern-day Siena.

The **Baptistery** lies below the apse of the Cathedral, where the so-called "Sabatelli Steps" (1451) lead down to Piazza San Giovanni. The upper part of this baptismal church was never completed; its clearly-organized façade includes parts of the Cathedral's apse. Mighty columns, which also carry the weight of the Cathedral choir, support the frescoed ceiling. The font is a 15th-century masterpiece, sporting reliefs by Jacopo della Quercia, Donatello and Ghiberti, among others.

Within a portion of the walls of the never-completed "Nove Duomo," the **★Cathedral Museum** ⑩ (Museo dell' Opera) makes its home. This is also the entrance to the unfinished façade of the Duomo, which commands a wonderful view of Siena and the surrounding countryside. On the Museo's ground floor, you can see the originals of Pisano's sculptures for the Cathedral; but the showpiece

Above: Fifteen of San Gimignano's towers have survived.

is on the upper floor: the *Maestà* by Duccio di Buoninsegna. Painted on both front and back, this altarpiece, executed between 1308 and 1311, was honored after its completion with three days of festivities, and adorned the Cathedral's main altar for the next 200 years. It represents, in fact, the first masterpiece of the great age of Sienese painting in the 14th century. While the main image is still locked in the conventions of tradition, depicting a rigid figure of an enthroned Madonna against a background of gold and strictly symmetrical figures of saints, the smaller side panels depict scenes from the life of Christ with minute exactitude.

Back on the Piazza del Duomo, you can see, to the left of the Duomo, the Neo-Gothic, 18th-century Archbishop's Palace. Opposite it is the façade of the hospital, the *Spedale di Santa Maria delle Scale* ⑪, which was constructed as a hospice for pilgrims in the days of the Frankish Road, perhaps as early as the 9th century. The frescoes by Domenico di Bartolo (ca. 1440) in the "Pilgrims' Room" give us an impression of what medieval "welfare services" were like.

There's plenty to discover, and anyone who comes prepared to spend a little time will soon discover that the city, strict and forbidding at first glance, only begins to unfold its charms to someone who spends a few hours wandering around. Furthermore, the shopping here is good, whether you're in the market for handicrafts or culinary specialties such as wild boar salami, wine, olive oil or the famous Sienese *panforte*, a kind of hard fruitcake with almonds, all of which make excellent gifts as well as souvenirs.

Along the Via Cassia to San Gimignano

The Via Cassia (S 22) runs parallel to the Siena-Florence expressway and offers, as does the Via Chiantigiana (SS 222; also connected to the S 22), a chance to discover the Chianti wine country. An old Roman road, the Via Cassia offers wonderful panoramic views.

The word Chianti awakens associations even in those who have never been to Tuscany. It conjures up images of rolling hills, silvery olive groves, cypresses and, of course, vineyards. And nearly everyone has tasted Chianti wine at one time or another. In the 1960s and 70s, you could buy it in supermarkets for next to nothing in the famous *fiaschi*. Today, these straw-wrapped bottles are largely obsolete, and quality and prices have increased substantially. (See also "Chianti Wine" feature, p. 78.)

Heading northwest from Siena toward San Gimignano, the "City of Beautiful Towers" – or the "Manhattan of the Middle Ages," according to some – you take the Via Cassia to Poggibonsi. The route goes next in a westerly direction along the main road to Villa Pietrafitta and from there via a side road to San Gimignano (from Siena circa 40 kilometers).

★★SAN GIMIGNANO

The skyline of **★★San Gimignano** ⑭ is probably the most-photographed image in all of Tuscany. Correspondingly, the tourist traffic in the city and its immediate surroundings is intense, particularly on weekends and holidays, when even Italians swarm up the hill like locusts. One bit of advice: Rather than spend hours in traffic trying to make your way up to the overcrowded parking lots by the city walls, park your car lower down and take a beautiful walk across the fields toward the towers, which will serve as guideposts so that you can't lose your way.

San Gimignano is the medieval town *par excellence*; its 13th- and 14th-century structures remain practically unchanged. In the 10th century, this former Etruscan settlement took on the name of the canonized Bishop of Modena, San Gimignano, who was supposed to have saved it from a

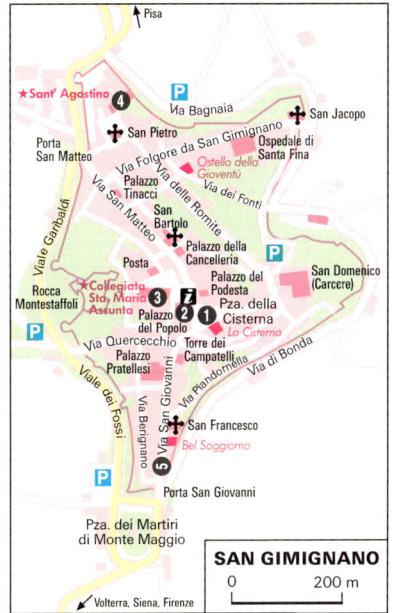

SAN GIMIGNANO

0   200 m

From Siena To Chianti

barbarian invasion. In 1199, the town became a *libero commune*, a city with its own independent government. As a free republic, it fought against other nearby cities, Volterra in particular. Inner power struggles divided the population into two camps, who followed either the Guelph Ardinghelli or the Ghibellinese Salvucci. However, the plague of 1348 devastated the city to such an extent that in 1354 it succumbed to Florence once and for all.

San Gimignano had developed into a trade center along the old Frankish Road, which was used by pilgrims on their way to Rome as early as the 8th century. The cultivation of saffron, which was used to color valuable silks, ensured the city's considerable wealth. Most of the important public buildings were constructed during the period of the republic, as were the residential towers of the town's leading families, which served, in effect, as miniature fortresses. In the 14th century, there were 72 such residential towers; 15 of these are left today. Important artists from Florence, Pisa, Lucca and Siena

were commissioned to decorate churches and homes. In the 13th century, a double ring of city walls was erected to protect the fortified town center and the districts of San Matteo and San Giovanni. Much of it still exists today.

San Gimignano (pop. 8,000) has not grown much since the Middle Ages, and can easily be explored in a day. At the center of town is the **Piazza della Cisterna ❶**, with a magnificent fountain built in 1273, and Cathedral Square with the **Cathedral** (Duomo) and **Palazzo del Podestà**, both built in the 12th century. Arnolfo di Cambio is thought to be responsible for the **Palazzo del Popolo ❷**, decorated with armorial bearings, at the south end of the square. Completed in 1288, it now houses the municipal administration and civic museums. The tallest tower is that of the Town Hall, the Torre Grossa – after it was built, no one was allowed to construct anything taller. Most

Above: Fresco by Benozzo Fozzoli in San Gimignano's Cathedral.

of the private family towers which have survived stand around these two squares.

Worth seeing is the interior of the Romanesque **★Collegiata Santa Maria Assunta ❸** Cathedral (remodeled and expanded by Guiliano da Maiano in the 15th century), with works by Benozzo Gozzoli, Taddeo di Bartolo, Jacopo della Quercia and Barna da Siena. There are also two frescoes by Ghirlandaio in the chapel of Saint Fina.

The **Via San Matteo** leads from Cathedral Square to the Porta San Matteo. Not far from here is the church of a mendicant oder, **★Sant'Agostino ❹**, with 15th-century frescoes in glowing colors by Benozzi Gozzoli which show with great attention to detail scenes from the life of the Father of the Church, Augustine. On **Via San Matteo** and **Via San Giovanni ❺**, which connects Piazza della Cisterna with the Porta San Giovanni, you'll encounter the main stream of tourist traffic, and souvenir shops and restaurants catering to tourists line these two streets.

If you don't care for these supermarkets of "typical Tuscan products," and seek more meaningful impressions, you need only go a few steps further to experience the real, living San Gimignano. And at night, when the busloads of tourists have left, quiet returns to the town. If you then stand on the city walls or on the ruins of the old fortress and take in the breathtakingly beautiful landscape, you'll agree that this town has earned its reputation as one of the most beautiful in all Tuscany.

VOLTERRA

About 10 kilometers south of San Gimignano you join to the main road No. 68, which 20 kilometers further west reaches **★Volterra ⓯** (pop. 16,000), situated atop a bare hill between the Cecina and the Era valleys. Here is a starker landscape, not planted with vineyards or olive groves, but rather divided up for grain fields and sheep pastures. The hill con-

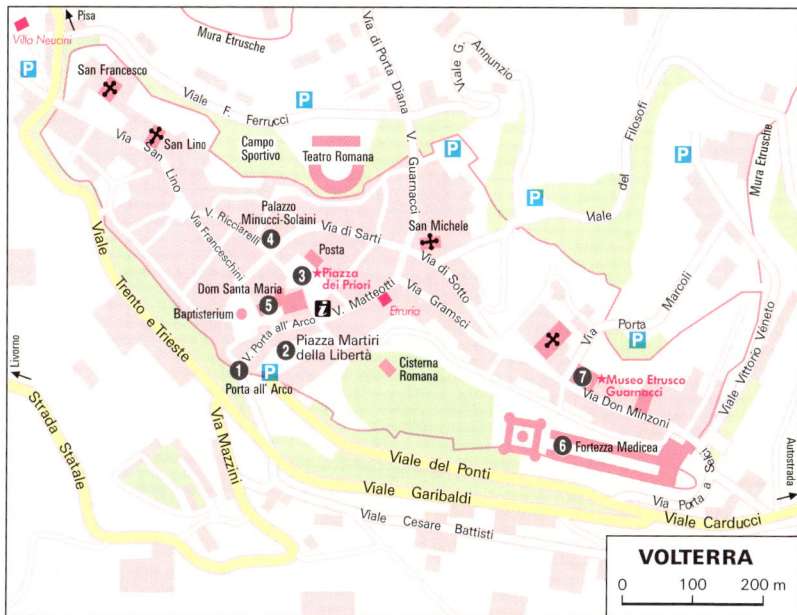

sists of clay and sandstone from the Pliocene period, and is subject to severe erosion. Landslides and mudslides are responsible for the "Balze," deep crevasses which have already swallowed up entire Etruscan necropolises. The ancient settlement of Badia, located outside of town, is also in danger of sliding into the depths.

The first settlements on this hill date back to the New Stone Age. After the Villanova period, these settlements united into a town that became one of the 12 members of the Etruscan League. Remnants of the wall enclosure, the **Porta all'Arco** ❶ adorned with mysterious heads (4th century B.C.), as well as the **Acropolis**, testify to the former importance of the one-time settlement of *Velathris*.

And don't omit a visit to one or two of the ★**alabaster workshops** clustered on the **Via Porta all'Arco** ❷ to watch the modern techniques of this originally Etruscan craft. Of course, much of what's produced today out of this half-transparent gypsum is tourist-oriented kitsch, but

you can occasionally find a pretty piece that makes a nice souvenir.

In the 3rd century B.C., the Etruscan city was incorporated into the Roman Empire. Its residents assumed the Christian faith early on, and by the time the Roman Empire fell, Volterra already had a Bishop and was a substantial diocese. From the 12th century on, the city was a free commune with its own independent government and laws, until it came under Florentine rule in the year 1472.

Today, Volterra is a quiet, contemplative town that has maintained much of its medieval character. At its center is the **Piazza dei Priori** ❸, considered to be one of the best-preserved medieval squares in all of Italy. The monumental **Palazzo dei Priori** proudly shows off the armorial bearings of its Florentine governors. Construction on this building began in 1208, making this the oldest Town Hall in Tuscany.

On the other side of the piazza stands the 13th-century **Palazzo Pretorio**, with its battlemented *Torre del Porcellino*, or

Above: Even in the days of the Etruscans, craftsmen tooled alabaster in Volterra.

Piglets' Tower. The medieval **tower houses**, such as those of the families Buonparenti and Bonaguidi on Via Buonparenti west of the Piazza dei Priori, contribute to the city's architecturally homogeneous appearance, a medieval flair which managed to withstand even the architectural improvements and additions of the Renaissance. The **Palazzo Minucci-Solaini** ❹ (northwest of the Piazza), for example, fits harmoniously between the medieval tower residences.

The Romanesque **Cathedral** ❺ and Baptistery are situated on the Piazza San Giovanni, just a few steps further on. Far more interesting than the exterior of the Cathedral are the artworks inside, such as the marble ciborium on the altar; the angels supporting the candelabra at either side of the high altar, by Mino da Fiesole; the Romanesque pulpit; and a 13th-century wooden sculpture showing Christ being taken off the cross. A fresco by

Benozzo Gozzoli in the Cappella dell' Addolorata depicts the Adoration of the Magi. The octagonal green-and-white striped **Baptistery**, dating from 1284, has been restored and is open once again.

In Volterra you can also see ruins from the ancient world, such as the remains of the **Roman Theater** or the **Roman Baths**. At the highest point of the city stands the mighty **Citadel** ❻, the so-called *Maschio*, which Lorenzo the Magnificent had built for defense purposes. Today, this gigantic Renaissance building serves as a prison and can, unfortunately, only be viewed from a distance. From the lovely park in front of the castle, however, you can take in the full effect of this impressive edifice.

In Volterra, don't miss the Etruscan **Museo Etrusco Guarnacci** ❼, which has grown out of the substantial private collection which Mario Guarnacci, a local prelate and scholar, donated to the city in 1761. The museum displays several of the most significant Etruscan artifacts found in the Volterra region.

SIENA (☎ 0577)

ℹ️ Piazza del Campo 56, tel. 280551, fax 270676.

🏨 🌑🌑🌑 **Certosa di Maggiano**, Via di Certosa 82, tel. 288180, fax 288189. **Park Hotel**, Via Marciano18, tel. 44803, fax 49020. **Villa Patrizia**, Via Fiorentina 58 tel. 50431, fax 50442.

🌑🌑 **Hotel Santa Caterina**, Via Piccolomini 7, tel. 221105, fax 271087. **Antica Torre**, Via Fieravecchia 7, tel./fax 222255. **Duomo**, Via Stalloreggi 38, tel. 289088, fax 43043. **Residence Fattoria di Catignano**, Loc. Catignano, tel. 356744, fax 356755.

🌑 **Piccolo Rotei Il Palio**, Piazza del Sale 19, tel. 281131, fax 281142. **Bernini**, Via della Sapienza, 15, tel./fax 289047.

YOUTH HOSTEL: **Guidoriccio**, Via Fiorentina 89, Loc. Stellino, tel. 52212, fax 055-8050104.

🔺 **Siena Colleverde**, Strada di Scacciapensieri 47, tel. 280044, fax 333298, open last week of March to first week of November, swimming pool. **Le Soline**, Casciano di Murlo, tel. 817410, fax 817415, 23 km south of Siena, open year round.

❌ **Antica Trattoria Botteganova**, Strada Chiantigiana (towards Gaiole) 29, tel. 284230. Classic Tuscan cuisine from local products, reasonable prices, closed Mon. **Mariotti da Mugolone**, Via dei Pellegrini 6/8, tel. 283235. In city center, good Sienese cuisine, delicious pastries for dessert. Closed Thu. **Al Marsili**, Via del Castoro 3, tel. 47154. In the Old Town, closed Mon. **La Torre**, Via Salicotti 7, tel. 287548. Modest trattoria, reasonable prices. Closed Thu.

🏛️ *MUSEUMS:* **Cathedral Museum**, mid-March to Sept 9 am to 7:30 pm, Oct 9 am to 6 pm. Nov to mid-March 9 am to 1:30 pm. **Libreria Piccolomini** (in Cathedral), mid-March to Oct 9 am to 7:30 pm; Nov to mid-March 7:30 am to 1:30 pm and 2:30 to 5 pm. **Pinacoteca Nazionale**, Palazzo Buonsignori, Via S. Pietro 29. Summer: Mon 8:30 am to 1:30 pm, Tue-Sat 9 am to 7 pm, Sunday/holidays 8 am to 1:30 pm. Winter: Tue-Sat 8:30 am to 1:30 pm and 2:30 to 5:30 pm, Sunday/holidays 8 am to 1 pm. Closed Jan 1, May 1 and Dec 25.

SIGHTS: **Palazzo Comunale** and **Tower of Town Hall**, Piazza Del Campo. Winter Mon-Sat 10 am to 4 pm; in summer Mon-Sat 10 am to 6 pm; July-Aug 10 am to 11 pm; Sun/hol 9:30 am to 1:30 pm; closed on Jan 1, May 1 and Dec 25.

CHURCHES: **Cathedral**, same hours as Libreria Piccolomini.

🍷 **Enoteca Italiana**, Fortezza Medicea, stocks over 600 varieties of wine. **Fattoria del Gallo Nero**, Via Sapienza 35, excellent Chianti wines. **Food market**, Piazza del Mercato, Tue-Sat, mornings only.

SAN GIMIGNANO (☎ 0577)

ℹ️ **Associazione Pro Loco**, Piazza del Duomo 1, tel. 940008, fax 940903.

🏨 🌑🌑 **La Cisterna**, Piazza della Cisterna 24, tel. 940328, fax 942080. Converted monastery in town center, attractive rooms decorated in 18th-century Florentine style. **Bel Soggiorno**, Via San Giovanni 91, tel. 940375, fax 943149. Beautiful 13th-century building with attractive, cozy rooms, own restaurant with country views. **Villa Baciolo**, Loc. San Donato, tel. 942233, fax 942233. Four km south of San Gimignano, medieval country house surrounded by vineyards and olive groves. **Le Renaie**, Loc. Pancole, tel. 955044, fax 955126. Simple country hotel with pool and tennis courts.

YOUTH HOSTEL: **Ostello della Gioventù**, Via delle Fonti 1, tel. 941991, fax 8050104. No youth hostel card required, no age limit.

🔺 **Il Boschetto**, Loc. S. Lucia, tel. 940352, fax 941982. Pretty location, 2 km south of town.

❌ **Osteria del Carcere**, Via del Castello 13, tel. 0577-941905.Tuscan cuisine, closed Wed.

🍷 *WINE:* **Montenidoli**, southeast of town, tel. 941565.

VOLTERRA (☎ 0588)

ℹ️ **A.P.T.**, Via Turazza 2 (left at the Palazzo dei Priori), tel./fax 86150.

🏨 🌑🌑🌑 **San Lino**, Via San Lino 26, tel. 85250, fax 80620, luxury accommodation in a former nunnery.

🌑🌑 **Villa Nencini**, Borgo San Stefano 55, tel. 86386, fax 80601. **Etruria**, Via G. Matteotti 32, tel./fax 87377. **Nazionale**, Via dei Marchesi 11, tel. 86284, fax 84097, Volterra's oldest hotel (built in 1890). **Vecchio Mulino**, 9 km outside of town, on the edge of Saline di Volterra, tel./fax 44060, country house with only nine rooms, good food.

❌ **Trattoria del Sacco Fiorentino**, Piazza XX Settembre 18, tel. 88537. Classical Tuscan cuisine in tasteful surroundings, closed Wed. **La Tavernetta**, Via Guarnacci 14, tel. 87630. Good food, low prices. Closed Thu.

🏛️ **Museo Etrusco Guarnacci**, Via Don Minzoni. Mid-Oct to mid-March daily 9 am to 2 pm, otherwise daily 9 am to 7 pm. Museo d'Arte Sacra, Via Rama. Summer daily 9:30 am to 1 pm and 3 to 6:30 pm; winter daily 9 am to 1 pm.

🍷 *ALABASTER WARE:* **Artigianato Locale**, Via Garnacci 33. **Società Cooperativa Artieri Alabastro**, Piazza dei Priori 5, also offers stone-cutting courses. **Laboratorio Rossi**, Via del Mandorlo.

From Siena To Chianti

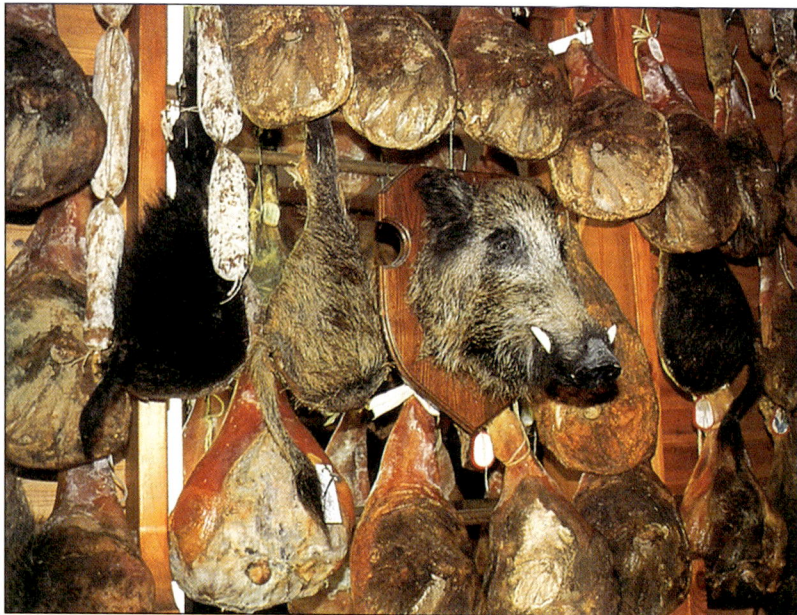

TUSCAN CUISINE

The same is true of Tuscany as of Italy in general: every region, every area has its own cuisine, based on whatever the local forests, fields or waterways happen to offer. For visitors, this is a guarantee that what you're served arrives fresh and without additives at your table. In general, one can say that traditional Tuscan cuisine is free of unnecessary refinement. It's simple cooking, a little on the frugal side, hearty and strongly spiced, so that it goes well with the unsalted bread that's served in abundance with every meal. The number of typical Tuscan recipes is rather limited. Olive oil is always a major ingredient; wild herbs, such as fennel or sage, are popular; and the region is known for its hearty soups and stews.

On the coast, there's plenty of fish available; predominant in the country's

Above: Wild boar delicacies. Right: A typical snack. Far right: Harvesting tomatoes can be a laborious task.

wooded interior are game dishes and different kinds of mushrooms. Vegetables are eaten everywhere, and every region has its own particular local specialty. The following is an attempt to introduce a few of these specialties and shed some light on how they're prepared.

Let's begin in northern Tuscany, in the green valleys of Garfagnana, where original grain types such as barley and spelt are still cultivated and used to produce hearty soups. Another typical dish here is made of cornmeal (*infarinata*), a thick stew enriched with beans, bacon and various vegetables, which is especially popular in the mountain country on cold winter nights.

Along the coast, fish is served in every imaginable manner. Particularly well-known are the *triglie alla livornese* from the coast of Livorno, which has the most fish of any area of Italy. For this dish, otherwise known as "red mullet, Livorno style," the fish are simmered slowly in a sauce of tomatoes, garlic and herbs, and served in the pan. Equally well-known,

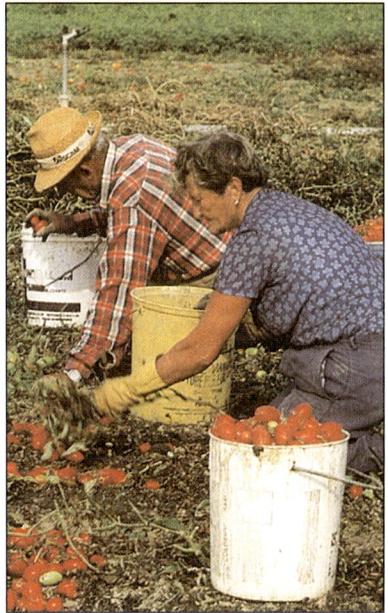

Cuisine

and equally popular, is the spicily-seasoned, creamy fish soup that goes by the name of *cacciucco*.

Every visitor to Florence is familiar with the word *bistecca*. This wonderfully tender, tasty piece of tenderloin comes from the white Chianina cattle from the Chiana Valley, which are bred solely for this rather tragic purpose. "Tragic" because the young animals of this fast-growing breed are slaughtered at the age of six or seven months, and they are confined exclusively to their stalls for the entire span of their brief lives. Nevertheless, their meat, cooked on the grill and drizzled with fine olive oil, is pure culinary poetry.

Typical of the area around Florence, but popular throughout Tuscany, are the white beans called *fagioli*, served in soups or as a side dish, drizzled with olive oil and perhaps garnished with a couple of slices of onion. A simple but tasty dish is *pappa al pomodoro*: old bread is softened in water and then mixed into a thick tomato soup.

Maremma is a region particularly blessed in its fertile earth, which, since the draining of its swamps about a century ago, has produced fruit and vegetables in abundance. The leanness of past years, however, can be seen from such holdovers as *acquacotta*, which translates as "cooked water," and proves on examination to be a soup of onions, eggs, vegetables, olive oil and toasted bread. A little *pecorino* (sheep's cheese), which is so excellent in this region that it's allowed to have its own protected label (DOC), is then grated over the soup

In the forests of the hinterland there is an abundance of game, wild mushrooms and chestnuts. Truffles are found in parts of the Maremma, and wild boar, above all, is served in every trattoria in a wide variety of dishes: roasted, as ham or salami, or as *salsiccia* (sausage). On the coast here, too, there is plenty of fresh fish, which in the evening, after your swim, you can buy directly from the men on the fishing-boats that have just come in for the night.

CHIANTI WINE
From Quantity to Quality

In the 1960s, bulbous, straw-covered bottles filled with Chianti wine, the characteristic *fiaschi*, flooded the shelves of supermarkets throughout the European Community. Back then, anyone who overindulged in Chianti in the evening ran the risk of experiencing a colossal hangover the next morning – and the Chianti vintners soon found that their fiaschi were something of a fiasco. In 1970, they produced a massive 240 million bottles, but they could hardly make the production pay off; the country was in the throes of radical social changes which were altering traditional farming structures and methods of cultivation. Some problems of this era persist to the present day, yet connoisseurs of good wine can still enjoy making new discoveries in Tuscany.

Tuscany's vast areas of cultivated land are comprised of a range of different soils and situations, and the vintners who try their luck here are of equally diverse skills and have differing senses of responsibility with regard to the quality of their products. Over the past decades the traditional vineyards, with their alternating rows of grapevines and olive trees, have practically disappeared; increasingly, the landscape is dominated by monotonous ranks of vineyards, a result of industrial production. These acres produce a veritable sea of wine each year. The products vary extremely in quality and character – from pale supermarket swill to fruity and well-balanced, top-quality products.

Strictly speaking, the historic region of Chianti is a small triangular area bordered by Florence, Arezzo and Siena (Chianti Classico, Chianti Colli Fiorentini). Today, however, the cultivable areas for Chianti extend south beyond Montepulciano (Chianti Colli Senesi), west to

Right: It's such grapes as these that yield the venerable Vino Nobile di Montepulciano.

Pistoia (Chianti Montalbano) and into the area between Pisa and Volterra (Chianti Colline Pisani). Chianti Rufina grows east of Florence. But not every Chianti is a true Chianti; the "real," typical Chianti wines grow in the historic Chianti area and in the Rufina region.

"You are in the world of Gallo Nero," roadside signs inform you as you drive south of Florence. The black rooster, a trademark of the Chianti League in the Middle Ages, is today the trademark of the consortium that markets "Chianti Classico." The beverage bearing this historic name is, however, a relatively recent invention. Not until about a hundred years ago did Baron Ricasoli, at his castle Brolio, hit upon the idea of blending red and white grapes: 65 to 70 percent Sangiovese, 5 to 10 percent Canaiolo and 25 percent white Trebbiano and Malvasia – proportions which the "DOCG" (*Di Origine Controllata e Garantita*) regulation stipulates today.

Because of its white wine content, Chianti genuinely matures early; the wine can be served as early as the March following the harvest. However, a vintner's real expertise, or lack of it, is demonstrated in his "Riserva" products, aged in a barrel for at least three years. A good Chianti can be recognized by its brilliant ruby red color, its fruitiness and its mild bouquet. Its proportion of white grapes give it a pleasant lightness despite its full body. Even in Tuscany, you can't be sure that every year will present you with a favorable wine-growing climate. Especially memorable was the excellent year 1990; other notable vintages are '83, '85, '88 and '91.

The DOCG marking has only partly solved the problem of regulating the quality of Chianti. The yield per hectare has been officially reduced, as has the percentage of white grapes in the mixture. The use of wines from other regions has been restricted, but not forbidden everywhere; using other grapes, such as Caber-

net, is permitted. The tangle of red tape and controlling bodies can surely accomplish a great deal, but there's one thing it still can't guarantee: a truly outstanding product from every vintner. Excellent Chiantis made according to the classic blend are produced by the same vintners who make first-rate wines from old varieties of Sangiovese grapes without the addition of any other variety. In every well-known wine-growing town you can get more information about local products at any *Enoteca*, and go on to taste them for yourself.

The fate of Ricasoli, the "inventor" of Chianti Classico, and his vineyard illustrates the situation of Chianti vineyards today. Sold to a beverage group in 1974, the vineyard was run into the ground, to be reclaimed by the Ricasoli family some years ago in a state of almost total ruin. The family is now trying to regain their former reputation. Another committed producer, Giovanella Stianti of Castello di Volpaia, is demonstrating one way to achieve success. She cultivates her vine-

yards "ecologically," without the use of artificial fertilizers and pesticides, and by systematically cultivating old grape varieties while preserving the tradition of mixed cultivation with olive trees. In addition to her traditional Chianti Classico, her Coltassala from Sangiovese grapes and her Balifico have become famous.

The same can be said for family businesses such as the small Fattoria Vigna Vecchia in Radda, run by Franco Beccari. In addition to his Chianti Classico Riserva, his Raddese is superb. Other vineyards which produce high-quality Chianti wines include Castellare and Castello di Fonterutoli, both near Castellina; Podere Il Palazzino near Gaiole; Vecchie Terre di Montefili near Greve; and Fattoria Isole e Olena in Barberino Val d'Elsa.

It is also worth visiting some of the less well-known Rufina wineries in the Sieve Valley, whose wines are robust and solid. Between Florence and Pistoia is the small wine-growing region of Carmignano, where an excellent red wine is pressed

from four classic Chianti grape varieties and an admixture of Cabernet Sauvignon.

The Vino Nobile di Montepulciano from the south of Tuscany is, on the other hand, produced like a Chianti; but the Montepulciano wines come out rather poorly in comparison with the best Chiantis. It's not far from here, in the Montalcino area, that the unique Brunello is produced. In the 19th century, the Biondi-Santi wine growers began producing a wine from Sangiovese-Grosso grapes, aged in oak barrels. A Brunello needs at least four years to mature. Since the wine has recently become fashionable, countless suppliers have flooded the market, often with wines that don't quite conform to the strict principles of Biondi-Santi that made Brunello famous and guarantee its distinctive character. Accordingly, you should be that

Above: Most Tuscans purchase their wine from the vat. Right: Alabaster fruit and eggs – there's something in Volterra to suit every taste.

much more critical when considering this top-class wine. A few reliable vintners include Poggio Antico, Poderi Costanti in Colle al Matrichese, and the Fattoria of Nello Baricci in Colombaio di Montosoli.

In Chianti and other regions of Tuscany, vintners are experimenting with new varieties of grapes and types of wine. Yet these rather expensive products, often oriented toward a French taste, seem to lack the typical Tuscan element that characterizes a good Chianti. Nevertheless, committed and experimental young oenologists have come up with some surprisingly good wines in the past few years, often from areas previously thought of as mediocre. Examples of these are the excellent Sassicaia from Bolgheri and the award-winning red wine from the Fattoria Sorbaiano in Montecatini Val di Cecina in the Montescudaio region, west of Volterra. There is also a popular *vino frizzante*, sold under the bland name of Matre and produced by the cooperative of Capalbio from Malvasia and Trebbiano.

The region's white, ordinary table wines taste good at the local wine festivals, but they neither travel nor keep well. The Fattoria Buonamico and the Carmignani families in Montecarlo near Lucca produce good white wines; and there's also an excellent white in Pomino, east of Fiesole.

The better-known white wines made from the Vernaccia grape in the district around San Gimignano are generally of rather mediocre quality. One of the few exceptions is the Vernaccia made by Fattoria Ponte a Rondolino. A *bianco* is also produced around Cortona and in the far south near Pitigliano.

Finally, you shouldn't pass up the opportunity to take along a bottle of *vin santo*, an excellent dessert wine similar in taste to sherry. Remember: it is difficult to find truly good products. A few reliable examples, though, are Avignonesi in Montepulciano, Castello di Volpaia and Isole e Olena in Barberino Val d'Elsa.

ARTS AND CRAFTS

To see Florence differently, for once! Not, in the usual manner, to follow the stations of great artists, painters, sculptors or architects, but rather to seek out the *artigiani*, the artisans. Since the Middle Ages, they have ensured that Florence be known far and wide for its crafts and applied arts; together with the merchants, they helped ensure the city's reputation and wealth. By the end of the 12th century, the city's artisans were already forming guilds to help regulate production and trade. And these guilds quickly came to exercise political power, something demonstrated, for example, by the Weavers' Revolt of 1378, which helped a member of the still-unknown Medici family to take political office for the first time. At the same time, the guilds acted as commissioners and patrons of public projects, playing an important role in the city's cultural and artistic development.

Wandering through Florence, you encounter traces of this past everywhere.

Take the church of Orsanmichele, a former granary which the guilds transformed into their temple and meeting-place. Countless streets and piazzas bear the names of old guilds or professions; the *Palazzo dell'Arte della Lana*, the guild house of the wool merchants, still stands on the Via Calimala; and many houses still bear the coats-of-arms of various professions over their doors.

The oldest guild in Florence was, in fact, that of the Calimala; its name derives from the street running between the old marketplace, now the Piazza Reppublica, and the Mercato Nuovo, where the members of the guild, mainly cloth traders, had their shops. Later, these wool traders moved into first place; at the end of the 13th century, they had more than 300 factories available to them and employed about a quarter of the city's population. The guild of Por Santa Maria, which at first included only dealers in dry goods and goldsmiths, didn't become powerful until the silk-makers joined its ranks; the most valuable product of the latter was brocade cloth, which was in great demand. The patterns on these fabrics were designed by such artists as Lippi, Botticelli and Ghirlandaio. Among the so-called "higher" guilds were those of the money-changers, the judges and notaries, doctors and pharmacists; the "middle" guilds included butchers, shoemakers, blacksmiths, tanners, stonemasons and carpenters. Other professions were lumped together in the "lower" category.

On your excursion into this Florentine past, you'll notice that the borders between artisans and artists often blur. Art and artisan guilds, *arte e arti*: even the Italian language doesn't make much of a distinction. Our separation of art as an intellectual, spiritual expression as opposed to the mechanical workmanship of artisans is a relatively modern development. In the days of Leonardo da Vinci, art was not produced in studios, but rather in workshops; painting and sculpture counted as "applied," rather than "fine," arts. Such artists as Michelangelo, Giotto and Ghirlandaio were simply the best in their guilds. Sculptor Andrea Verrocchio created monumental sculptures, but also banners for tournaments; the painter Botticelli earned extra money by decorating dowry chests; and Donatello, like nearly all the sculptors of his day, trained not as a sculptor, but as a goldsmith.

Today, throughout Florence, you can watch the descendants of these great masters, recipients of artisan wisdom that have been passed down from generation to generation, as they work wood, stone or metal according to the original old methods. They are masters of the traditional techniques, know all of the ins and outs of their trade, and can make old things look new or new things old. For a long period, Florence's artisans contented themselves with merely copying the venerated objects of the past; today,

however, it's once again difficult to draw the distinction between artist and artisan. These women and men, often true masters of their trade, are again employing traditional techniques in conjunction with modern shapes and forms: the resulting objects are true works of art(isanship).

Don't put off paying a visit to a traditional workshop. Even though there are still masterful artisans, industrial production is inevitably taking over, and the traditional techniques are slowly dying out. And fewer and fewer young artisans are coming along to take up the torch. But for the time being, production continues, both in Florence and throughout Tuscany. There's a particular flurry of activity in the streets around Santa Croce and Santo Spirito, neighborhoods which it was once advisable to frequent only in broad daylight. Legion small workshops here build new furniture or restore old pieces; carve and gild picture frames; repair musical instruments; weave or sew fabric; throw ceramics. The air is filled with the smells of clay and glue, paint and wax.

In the alleyways to the left and right of the Arno, too, you can find artisans who make objects to order or ably repair broken porcelain and ceramic heirlooms with patience and skill. Some have even achieved world renown, such as the woodcarver Bartolozzi on Via Maggio, who with the help of a few photographs was able to recreate the choir pews of the Benedictine monastery of Monte Cassino after it was destroyed in World War II.

And before you know it, your tour has become a shopping expedition. One typical souvenir of Florence is stone inlay work. With the old technique of *pietre dure*, a paste of powdered gum resin, marble and shell is used to create marvelous patterns in stone. There are also true artists among the ranks of potters, who use their wheels to create marvelous traditional or modern ceramics.

On the Ponte Vecchio, you can see the monument which the old guild of the

Right: Florentine artisanship has long enjoyed an excellent reputation.

goldsmiths erected to their great master Benvenuto Cellini – perhaps in part to remind themselves of the great creative heights to which members of their profession can rise. Where today gold is melted, shaped and soldered was, until the 16th century, a base for the city's butchers. Because of the stench of their waste, which they threw into the Arno, they were forced to clear the site and move further out of town.

Near the water, too, are the city's leather tanneries, where, now as in the past, leather is tanned, cut, gilded, chased and transformed into elegant boxes or book covers.

If you would like to see how *carta marmorizzata*, the marbled paper so typical of Florence, has been produced for centuries, you can go to Giannini on the Piazza Pitti and watch the bizarre patterns forming atop a tank of water. In the neighboring quarter of San Frediano is the *Antico Setificio Fiorentino*, where marvelous silk fabrics are produced on traditional looms.

Pescia attracts visitors with its large flower market and with handmade copper wares. If you have the time and can speak Italian, the maestro Giovanni Donnini, by the Porta Fiorentina, will doubtless be more than happy to explain to you the secrets of his trade. Before it's altogether too late and people have quite forgotten the traditional artisan methods, the town of San Gimignano, where cabinet-making and embroidery are the main crafts, has opened a museum of these trades. Hand-crafted lace and crossbows are the signature products of Sansepolcro, city of Piero della Francesca.

What's the difference between a Florentine, Neapolitan and Sardinian knife? In Scarperia, north of Florence, you'll surely find an expert who can give you the answer. And in Volterra, you can see that Tuscany's artisan traditions still bear an Etruscan stamp. After visiting the museum with antique alabaster urns, you can go into the shop of a modern craftsman and see how he still works this "stone of light" from the belly of the earth.

METRIC CONVERSION

Metric Unit	US Equivalent
Meter (m)	39.37 in.
Kilometer (km)	0.6241 mi.
Square Meter (sq m)	10.76 sq. ft.
Hectare (ha)	2.471 acres
Square Kilometer (sq km)	0.386 sq. mi.
Kilogram (kg)	2.2 lbs.
Liter (l)	1.05 qt.

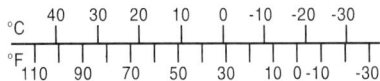

°C 40 30 20 10 0 -10 -20 -30
°F 110 90 70 50 30 10 0 -10 -30

TRAVEL PREPARATIONS

When to Go

Tuscany is "in season" all year long. More than four million foreign and Italian tourists, who have more than 120,000 beds in hotels and pensions at their disposal, flood into Florence and other popular tourist centers throughout the year – above all on short package tours on holiday weekends. If possible, try to avoid planning a trip to Tuscany over Easter, Pentecost (Whitsuntide), or Christmas. It can also be unbearable in the cities in the oppressive heat of summer; at this time, you're better off following the lead of the Tuscans themselves, who set aside their work in July and August and take refuge at the seaside.

Another alternative is to seek out the cooler regions up in the mountains, where you can go off for marvelous hikes, but where you'll find that there's still, often as not, plenty of diversion for lovers of art and culture.

The mild Mediterranean climate makes Tuscany particularly marvelous in spring and autumn. As most visitors, however, think the same way, it may be quite difficult to find lodging in these seasons. It can also happen that a visitor in April/May or October/November may be surprised by a sudden cloudburst. Seldom, however, will you encounter a protracted period of bad, rainy weather, such as you might expect to find north of the Alps.

Art lovers, more than anyone else, are well advised to travel in winter, when the museums are likely to be empty of people. The countryside, too, has a special attraction all its own at this time of year. At higher altitudes, however, January may see temperatures around freezing level, and the old stone buildings can get extremely cold. Particularly in mid- to low-priced accommodations, the heating is often inadequate for the winter weather.

If you want to take the time to get to really know Tuscany rather than merely stopping in for a superficial visit, you should plan to stay for at least three weeks. If you don't have that much time, then limit yourself to fewer destinations; for Tuscany is a land that demands time, effort, and a sense of adventure if you want truly to get to know it.

What to Wear

Light summer clothes are always fine, but in spring and autumn you should be sure to bring along a warm sweater and some rain gear. In winter, you'll probably need warm woollen clothing. And it's not a bad idea to take along a blanket or a sleeping bag, which may stand you in good stead as extra bedding in old country estates or hotels and pensions in the lower price category.

When visiting churches and monasteries, make sure you're wearing suitable clothing: no shorts and no mini-skirts, and keep your shoulders covered. If you don't follow this code, they may not let you in. Italians set store by dressing well and, above all, properly. Even in beach towns, therefore, don't run around in your bathing suit unless you don't mind being followed by disapproving glances.

Tuscany in Figures

Tuscany is the fifth-largest of the 20 regions of Italy. It measures about 23,000 square kilometers and is divided into 10 provinces: Arezzo, Florence, Grosseto, Livorno, Lucca, Massa-Carrara, Pisa, Pistoia, Prato (since 1993) and Siena.

The largest cities (1999 census) are Florence (377,000), Livorno (162,000), Prato (171,000) and Pisa (93,000).

Quite some time ago, Tuscany ceased to be primarily an agricultural region: today, less than 10 percent of the population makes a living from agriculture, although the figure is 20 percent in the provinces of Siena and Grosseto. The main crops are grains, feed plants, wine and olives; there is also some cultivation of fruits and vegetables. Other agricultural products are meat, sheep's-milk cheese and tobacco.

Some 60 percent of all Tuscans are employed in the industrial sector (engineering and textile industries, shoemaking, woodworking and chemical industries) or support themselves by artisan skills, usually practiced in small or family businesses. Trade and service fields (mainly in the tourist industry) support about one-quarter of the population. One-tenth of all tourists in Italy head for Tuscany; of these, about 35 percent are foreigners, 40 percent Italians and 25 percent Tuscans.

Crime

Tourist centers can be hotspots of criminal activity: be especially watchful of pickpockets, who might try to engage you in trivial conversation while relieving you of your wallet and jewelry. Even the seemingly innocent eyes of children are not necessarily to be trusted: bands of young thieves can be especially innovative in their methods. Use attended parking lots whenever possible, and never leave anything of value visible inside the car. It is a good idea to empty out the glove compartment and leave it open.

GETTING THERE

By Plane

Florence has its own international airport – Peretola. Peretola is also important for domestic connecting flights, and the expansion of the airport has begun. From abroad, you can also fly directly into Milan and continue on from there into Tuscany by train.

By Car

From Central Europe, if you're coming through Germany and Austria, you can get to Tuscany by taking the Autobahn A 22 and going by way of Bolzano, Verona and Modena. From there, the A 1 leads on via Bologna to Florence. If you're coming from the south (Rome), the A1 will also bring you to Florence, but from the other direction.

If you're driving in by way of southwest Germany or Switzerland, pick up the A 1 in Milan and follow it to Modena. You can also opt for the route from Milan-Parma, from where you can take the A 15 over the Cisa Pass to La Spezia and then get onto the A 12 to go further south. From Viareggio, the cross land route A 11 (Firenze-Mare) runs through Lucca and on to Florence.

If you're coming from France, follow the A 12, which leads from Genoa along the scenic Ligurian coast and then through the Versilia to Pisa or Livorno. You're required to pay a toll for the privilege of traveling on an Italian expressway. From the Brenner Pass to Florence, the charge (latest info 1999) is about 60,000 lire. The purchase of a Viacard for 50,000 lire, available at expressway gas stations, is recommended. There are special lanes for card users at the exits.

Avoid at all costs driving on the second weekend of August: during *Ferragosto*, the Italian vacation weekend, traffic jams are of monumental proportions.

By Train

Florence is situated on one of the main Italian train lines, and therefore has direct connections to a number of European cities. A number of trains end at the dead-end station of Santa Maria Novella in

Guidelines

Florence; trains which go on from Florence stop at the station Campo di Marte in the eastern part of the city.

If you want to travel to your final destination by taking a local train from one of the larger cities, then you'd better bring plenty of patience, as most of these trains really do stop at every station. This leisurely pace can, on the other hand, allow you some enchanting insights into provincial life.

By Bus

There aren't any regular international bus connections to Tuscany, but a number of private bus companies do offer package tours to Florence and Tuscany.

TRAVELING IN TUSCANY

If you're planning a tour of Tuscany's cities and know where you'd like to go, it's wisest to travel by plane or train. Most of the old city centers are closed to car traffic, parking lots can be few and far between and, furthermore, most of the sights, which are generally grouped together within a city center, are easy to reach on foot. Good public transportation within the cities, i.e., public buses, make it quick and easy to get to slightly out-of-the-way destinations. But if you'd like to get to know the region, and aren't prepared to hike or cycle an inordinate amount, you're practically obliged to go by car, which will give you the freedom to seek out small villages and hidden corners. Another advantage of going by car is that it gives you more room to transport wine, olive oil and any other specialties you might want to stock up on.

Of course, you can always rent a car (or motorcycle) in Tuscany, as well. All major rental car companies have branches in Florence and the region's other large cities. It is considerably cheaper if you make a reservation in advance.

There are also three main bus networks in Tuscany, operated by the transport companies SITA, CAP and Lazzi Fratelli. In addition, smaller local buses service individual cities and the surrounding villages. You can buy tickets at the bus company offices or in bars and kiosks in town.

PRACTICAL TIPS

Accommodation

Hotels: Hotels and pensions in Italy are classified or categorized by stars (* to ****). This system, however, doesn't take into account the location, possible noise, or atmosphere. Still, you can assume that a three-star hotel (☉☉) will provide solid comfort at moderte prices. Anything over that is luxury class (☉☉☉) or first category, in which you can expect to pay as much as 350,000 (single) and 550,000 lire (double), and at least 150,000 (single) and 200,000 lire (double). In the lower price classes, accommodations can range from friendly little family hotels to run-down dumps. An adapter for personal electrical appliances (shaver, hair dryer) is usually necessary.

All in all, you can expect that in tourist centers such as Florence and Siena you'll have to pay more than you would elsewhere. Prices must be posted in the room and at the reception desk; breakfast is normally only served (at a charge) if the guest has asked for it. Usually, it's better to forget about the generally inadequate hotel breakfast and have a cappuccino and fresh *cornetto* (croissant) in the nearest bar.

There is reasonably priced, and often especially lovely and peaceful, accommodation in a number of old monasteries, where the food is often very good, as well. Sometimes, however, unmarried couples will not be allowed to share a double room in these facilities. *Agritourismus* ("Farmhouse Holidays") offers reasonably-priced accommodation. Complete hotel listings are available from A.P.T. offices or from local tourist information (Pro Loco) offices.

Youth Hostels: If you hold an international youth hostel membership card, you can sleep cheaply in Italian youth hostels. It's a good idea to call ahead, and essential if you're traveling in a group of more than five people. If the hostel is full, the maximum stay is three nights. For further information, contact the Associazione Italiana Alberghi per la Gioventù, Via Cavour 44, 00184 Rome, tel. 06-487-1152, fax 488-0492.

Camping: Most campgrounds in Tuscany are only open from April to September or October. You can make reservations through: Federcampeggio, Casella Postale 23, 50041 Calenzano, tel. 055-882391, fax 882-5918 . There, or at a local bookstore, you can also get a guide to campgrounds in the region.

Airline Offices in Florence

ALITALIA, Piazza dell'Oro 1, tel. 055-27881; *BRITISH AIRWAYS*, Via Vigna Nuova 36r, tel. 055-218655; *MERIDIANA:* Lungarno Vespucci 28r, tel. 055-230-2314; *SABENA:* Via Palagio degli Spini 1, tel. 055-337-1201 or 301470 (airport); *TWA*, Via Vecchietti 4, tel. 055-284691.

Banks

Banks in Italy are open Monday through Friday from 8:30 a.m. to 1:30 p.m. and – generally – from 3 to 4 p.m. At the Santa Maria Novella train station in Florence, the exchange counters are open longer, and are also open on Saturdays. Many hotels will change money for you, but the exchange rate is often much less favorable than it may be in exchange offices or banks. It's still cheapest to get the cash you need from automatic bank tellers with international card capacity, which are available in most medium-sized and large cities.

You can only cash Eurocheques at a bank, and they have to be filled out in lire in the presence of the teller. Many hotels and shops also take credit cards.

Breakdown Service

ACI (Automobile Club Italiano): 116

Bus Companies

SITA: Florence, Via Santa Caterina da Siena 17r, tel. 055-294955; **Lazzi Fratelli**: Florence, Piazza Stazione, tel. 055-351061.

Business Hours

In general, stores are open Monday to Saturday from 9 a.m. to 1 p.m., and from 4 or 5 until 7 or 8 p.m. Grocery stores close in winter on Wednesday afternoons and in summer on Saturday afternoons. In tourist centers, some stores have started abandoning the midday lunch break.

Car Rental (*Autonoleggio*)

FLORENCE (Area Code 055): **Avis**, airport, tel. 315588; Borgo Ognissanti, 128r, tel. 213629. **Program**, Borgo Ognissanti 135r, tel. 282916; **Europcar**, airport, tel. 318609; **Hertz Italiana Rent-a-Car**, Via Maso Finiguerra 33, tel. 282260; **Maggiore Autoservizi**, Via Maso Finiguerra 31r, tel. 210238; Via Termine 1, tel. 311256.
SIENA (Area Code 0577): **Avis**, Via Martini 36, tel. 270305. **Hertz**, Via XXIV Maggio 10, tel. 45085

Consulates in Florence

UK, Lungarno Corsini 2, tel. 284133 or 212594; **US**, Lungarno A. Vespucci 38, tel. 2398276 or 217605.

Electricity

It is recommended to bring along an adapter for electrical devices such as hair dryers and electric razors.

Emergency Numbers

Carabinieri: 112
Police and Emergencies: 113

Farmhouse Holidays

Agriturismo and *Turismo Verde:* Nowhere else do you have so many chances

Guidelines

to spend a relaxed, back-to-nature holday as you do in Tuscany. Countless former or still-working farmhouses offer reasonably-priced accommodation, often in the form of self-contained apartments. This may be with or without direct contact with the host family. If you want, you can also pay a small fee and have meals included as part of the package. Meals are taken with the family, and usually consist of good solid home fare made of the farm's own products.

For addresses and information, contact the local tourist information offices.

Information

Website of the Italian State Tourist Office **ENIT:** http://www.mi.cnr.it/WOI/.

In Canada: 3 place Ville Marie, 56 Plaza, Montreal H3B 2E3, tel. (514) 866-7667.

In the US: 630 Fifth Avenue, New York, NY 10111, tel. (212) 245-4822.

In Tuscany (A.P.T. or **Pro Loco):** Addresses and phone numbers are listed in the *INFO* sections at the end of every chapter.

Lost and Found Offices

You can get the addresses of lost and found offices (*Uffici oggetti smarriti*) from local tourist offices, at the Town Hall, or from various police offices (*Vigili urbani*). Lost property offices are open mornings only from 8 or 8:30 a.m. to about 1 p.m.

If you've left something lying in a public bus, train or ferry, go to the responsible authority (i.e., the railroad, bus company, or ferry line).

Medical Assistance

If you can present form E-111 entitling you to international medical treatment, **USL** (*Unità Sanitaria Locale*) centers will treat you free of charge. It's a good idea, however, to look into special travel insurance, particularly if you'd like to ensure a slightly better level of care.

In emergencies, call First Aid (tel. 118) or *Pronto Soccorso* at the hospital nearest you, as well as at train stations, harbors and airports.

Museums

Opening hours of museums are not regulated in Italy, and therefore tend to change frequently, which makes it difficult to state anything definite here. Most museums are closed at midday, from around 1 to 3 p.m., and some are only open in the morning. In many cases they close all day Monday. Many museums are closed on January 1, Easter Sunday, May 1 and December 25. To ensure that you don't end up standing in front of a locked door, phone ahead to check the opening hours, or ask at the local tourist office.

At present, admission fees for Italian museums are divided into three categories. The largest – including the Uffizi Gallery in Florence – now cost a uniform fee of 12,000 lire. Entrance to less spectacular establishments costs 8,000 lire, while the smallest museums charge 4,000 lire. Sometimes tickets valid for several mueseums are available (e.g., municipal museums in Florence). Check at the tourist information office.

Pharmacies

Opening hours of pharmacies are no different from those of other businesses. For information about opening times on Sundays and holidays, call the toll-free number 800-420707. In Florence, there are a few pharmacies with 24-hour service (area code 055): **All'Insegna del Moro**, Piazza S. Giovanni 20r, tel. 211343; **Comunale 5**, Piazza Isolotto 5, tel. 710293; **Comunale 13**, Stazione S. Maria Novella, tel. 289435; **Molteni**, Via Calzaiuoli, 7r, tel. 289490.

Post Office

Open Monday through Friday, usually from 8:15 a.m. to 1:40 p.m., Saturdays until 12:20 pm.

Shopping

Tuscany is a true shoppers' paradise for anyone looking for novel souvenirs, high-quality crafts, jewelry and antiques, or culinary delicacies.

Florence is clearly the shopping center of the region. For elegant fashion, the best place to look is the Via dei Tornabuoni, Via degli Strozzi and Via dei Calzaiuoli. There are also countless new boutiques, as well as leather and shoe shops and knitwear shops throughout the Old Town, as well as on the other side of the Ponte Vecchio. Here, in the alleyways around Santo Spirito, you'll find most of the city's traditional artisan workshops and restorers. The Ponte Vecchio itself is a center for gold- and silversmiths.

The famous *carta marmorizzata*, marbled paper colored according to centuries-old techniques, is another product of a traditional Florentine craft which you can buy all over the city, including the square of the Duomo. The lovely old pharmacy of Santa Maria Novella, Via della Scala 16, sells creams and soaps, liqueurs and perfumes made according to traditional recipes handed down by Dominican monks (for tips and addresses, see "Shopping in Florence," p. 38).

Volterra is known for its alabaster; countless workshops in the town produce a variety of objects either copied from old models or in wholly new forms. There's a lot of kitsch sold here, but if you seek out the smaller shops in the Old Town, you may find something pretty or original. In the city center, there's also a sales outlet for the Union of Artisan Alabaster Workers on the Piazza dei Priori 5, tel. 0588-87590.

Culinary delicacies are to be found throughout Tuscany. Some typical offerings include baked goods and spicy cakes, such as *panforte* from Siena, a dense kind of fruitcake prepared with honey and almonds, or the *Biscotti di Prato*, hard little cookies flavored with almonds and aniseed, which are a popular dessert, especially when they're dunked in *vin santo*.

Typical Tuscan cheese is generally made of sheep's milk (*pecorino*). You can purchase olive oil directly from the producer at many regional farmhouses. If the label announces that it's *Olio Extra Vergine d'Oliva*, and the contents are slightly cloudy and greenish, then you know it's of the very highest quality and worth the generally high price.

Many monasteries have pharmacies or sales outlets where they sell olive oil, honey, herbal liqueurs and cosmetics, all prepared by the monks or nuns according to traditional recipes.

Taxis

Florence: 4390.

Telephones

You can call from public telephone booths with coins or phone cards (*scheda telefonica*). Many bars have a public telephone you can use (you'll know it by the yellow telephone symbol posted by the door). The Italian phone company Telecom Italia (which is wholly independent of the post office) has some public rooms in larger towns which are fitted out with several phone booths, from which you can also make international calls. Furthermore there are private telephone companies, such as Infostrada, Tiscali and others which offer prepaid telephone cards with which charges for international calls are considerably cheaper. Most public telephones today have slots for coins and phone cards. You can buy phone cards at tobacconists or newspaper kiosks for 5,000, 10,000 and up to 100,000 lire. Please note: Even for local calls you need to dial the local area code; for calls from abroad, too, you must dial the zero of the area code.

Country code for Italy: +39.

Country codes (dialing from Tuscany): To the US and Canada 001; to the UK 0044; to Ireland: 00353.

Guidelines

Directory assistance: Domestic tel. 12; international tel. 176.

Thermal Baths

Tuscany has a wealth of mineral springs, most of which were already known in Antiquity. Today, the largest baths are Chianciano Terme and Montecatini Terme, but there are a dozen or so smaller spas. You can get information materials from local tourist offices. The following spas are about 100 kilometers from Florence:

Monsummano Terme: Grotta Giusti, Via Grotta Giusti 171, tel. 0572-51008; Grotta Parlanti, Via Grotta Parlanti 41b, tel. 953029.

Montecatini Terme: Viale Giuseppe Verdi 41, tel. 0572-7781.

Tipping *(Mancia)*

Tips are included in hotel and restaurant bills, but it never hurts to round up and add 5-10 percent of the total as a *mancia*. In bars, service is not included, so you should leave a 15 percent gratuity behind. Porters, too, expect you to round up; and you generally leave about 500 lire in attended toilets. At the cinema or theater, it's common practice to give the usher a tip of 500 to 1,000 lire.

Trade Fairs and Markets

Flower Markets: In Florence, Thursday mornings on Via Pellicceria. Every year at the end of April/beginning of May on the Piazza della Libertà there's a huge sales show of spring flowers. In Pescia, Tuscany's largest flower market is held Monday-Saturday from 6 to 9:30 a.m. (Via Salvo d'Aquisto).

There is a colorful flea market from Monday through Saturday in summer, Tuesday through Thursday in winter on the Piazza dei Ciompi in Florence. Local art and craft work can be found every third weekend on the Piazza d'Azeglio in Viareggio.

In Florence, every year from the end of April to the beginning of May, the International Artisan Congress (*Mostra Internazionale dell'Artigianato*) is held in the Fortezza da Basso. Distributors come from throughout Italy and from 30 other countries. For information, call 055-49721.

GLOSSARY OF FOOD AND DRINK

Though many menus are now written in English for the benefit of tourists, you may find the following glossary helpful in deciphering a Tuscan menu.

Food (*Cibi*)

acciughe . . . . sardines
aceto . . . . vinegar
acquacotta . . . . . . vegetable soup from the Maremma
affettato . . . . cold cuts
agnello . . . . lamb
aglio . . . . garlic
alici . . . . anchovies
anatra . . . . duck
anguria . . . . watermelon
arancia . . . . oranges
aragosta . . . . lobster
arrosto . . . . roast
baccalà . . . . stockfish, a specialty in Lunigiana
bistecca (ai ferri) . . . cutlet, beefsteak
bistecca fiorentina . . . juicy beefsteak from a Chianina calf
brodo . . . . consomé
bruschetta . . . . . . toasted bread with garlic and olive oil
burro . . . . butter
cacciucco . . . . . . Livornese fish soup
cantuccini . . . . . hard almond pastry, dunked in vin santo
caprese . . . . tomatoes with mozzarella
carciofi . . . . artichokes
castagnaccio . . . . . round, flat bread made of chestnut flour
cavolfiore . . . . cauliflower
cavolo con le fette . . . cabbage breads
cecina . . . . chick pea flat breads
cibreo . . . fricasseed chicken gizzards, a Florentine specialty

cinghiale . . . . wild boar	*noce*. . . . . nuts
coniglio . . . . rabbit	*orata* . . . . haddock
coda alla vacinara . . . . ox tail	*ossobuco* . . . . knuckle of veal
contorno . . . . side dish	with vegetables
costata. . . . . entrecôte	*ostriche* . . . . oysters
cozze . . . . mussels	*panforte*. . . . . very spicy cake from
crema. . . . . . cream, creamed soup	Siena, similar to gingerbread
crostata. . . . . fruit tart	*panino* . . . . bread roll
crostini . . . . roasted slices of white	*panna* . . . . heavy cream
bread with various herbs	*pappa al pomodoro* . . . . thick tomato
crudo . . . . raw	soup with bread
erbe . . . . herbs	*pasta e fagioli* . . . . thick noodle soup
fagiano. . . . . pheasant	with white beans
fagioli. . . . . white beans	*patate*. . . . . potatoes
fagioli all'uccelletto . . . . white beans	*pecorino* . . . . . sheep's-milk cheese
with lots of sage	*pepe* . . . . pepper
fagiolini . . . . green beans	*peperone* . . . . . sweet (bell) pepper
fegato. . . . . liver	*peperoncino* . . . . chili pepper
fegatelli . . . . liver kebab	*pera*. . . . . pear
fettunta . . . . . . toasted white bread	*pesce* . . . . fish
with garlic and olive oil	*pescespada* . . . . swordfish
finocchio . . . . fennel	*pesto*. . . . . basil sauce
finocchiona . . . . . thick salami with	*pinoli* . . . . pine nuts
fennel seeds	*piselli*. . . . . peas
formaggio . . . . cheese	*pizzaiola* . . . . . . spicy tomato sauce
francesina . . . . boiled meat dish	*pollo arrosto* . . . . roast chicken
frittata . . . . omelette	*pollo alla diavola* . . . . hot and spicy
fritto misto . . various types of fried fish	roasted chicken
funghi porcini. . . . . bolet mushrooms	*polpetta*. . . . . meat balls
gallina . . . . chicken	*pomodoro* . . . . tomatoes
gambero . . . . shrimps	*porchetta*. . . . . suckling pig
gnocchi. . . . . dumplings	*prosciutto*. . . . . ham
grano turco. . . . . corn	*ragù* . . . . meat sauce
grasso. . . . . lard	*riso* . . . . rice
infarinata. . . . . corn chowder	*rognoni* . . . . kidneys
involtini . . . . little meat rolls	*rognoncino* . . . . calf's kidneys
lampone . . . . raspberries	*rostinciana*. . . . . spareribs
lingua . . . . tongue	*sale* . . . . salt
lombata. . . . . tenderloin	*salmone* . . . . salmon
lumache. . . . . snails	*salsa (verde)* . . . . . . (green) sauce
maiale . . . . pork	*salsiccia* . . . . pork links
mandorla. . . . . almonds	*saltimbocca*. . . . . medaillon of calf
manzo. . . . . beef	with sage
mela . . . . apples	*scaloppine*. . . . . loin of veal
melanzane . . . . eggplant	*scottiglia* . . . . . pot roast including
menta. . . . . mint	various meats
merluzzo. . . . . cod	*seppia* . . . . squid
miele . . . . honey	*sogliola* . . . . sole
minestra . . . . soup	*spezzatino*. . . . . goulash

Guidelines

91

allo spiedo, spiedino . . . . kebab
spigola . . . . perch
succo. . . . . juice
sugo . . . . sauce
tacchino . . . . turkey
tartufo. . . . . . truffel (also ice cream)
tonno . . . . tuna
torta d'erbi . . . . herb tart
tramezzino . . . . sandwich
triglia. . . . . red mullet
triglie alla livornese . . . . . red mullet
à la Livornese
trippa alla fiorentina . . . . tripe
Florentine style
trota . . . . trout
in umido . . . . steamed
uovo. . . . . egg
uva . . . . grape
verdura . . . . vegetable
vitello. . . . . veal
vitello tonnato . . . . veal
with tuna sauce
vongole . . . . scallops
zucchero. . . . . sugar
zuppa di farro . . . . spelt soup

Drinks (*Bevande*)

acqua fresca . . . . drinking water
acqua gasata . . . . . carbonated water
amaretto . . . . . bitter-almond liqueur
amaro . . . . bitter digestive
aranciata. . . . . orangeade
bicchiere. . . . . glass
birra (alla spina) . . . . . beer (on tap)
caffè (espresso) . . . . espresso
caffèlatte. . . . . café au lait
cappuccino . . . . espresso with
foamed milk
ghiaccio . . . . ice cubes
grappa . . . . lees spirits
latte. . . . . milk
latte macchiato. . . . foamed milk with
a splash of coffee
mezzo litro, quarto di litro . . . . . .
half a liter, quarter of a liter
sambuca. . . . . aniseed liqueur
spremuta d'arancia, di limone,
di pompelmo . . freshly pressed orange,
lemon, grapefruit juice

Spumante . . . . sparkling wine
tè (al limone, con latte) . . . . . . tea
(with lemon, with milk)
vino abboccato, amabile . . sweet wine
vin santo . . . . . sweet dessert wine
vino secco . . . . dry wine

AUTHORS

Ulrike Bleek, Project Editor and co-author of this book, studied German literature and Romance languages and literature in Heidelberg, with a special focus on Italian literature. After several courses of study in Italy, she now works as a freelance television journalist and author in Munich. She is editor of the Italian editions of Nelles Guides. She was the Project Editor for the *Nelles Guide to Rome*, ("Around Florence," "From Siena to Chianti," "Tuscan Cuisine").

Christiane Büld-Campetti studied German and Dutch in Münster and Amsterdam, and has worked for 10 years as an editor for Bavarian Radio. For the past eight years, she has lived with her Florentine husband in an old farmhouse near Florence. From there, she provides a number of German radio stations with reports about the region and its people and contributions on cultural events in Tuscany.

Dr. Stephan Bleek studied history, political science and sociology in Munich, and has worked for many years as a television journalist and film author for Bavarian Television. Because one of his focuses is cultural history, he frequently travels to Italy, particularly to Tuscany. ("Arts and Crafts").

Kirsten Faber studied art history, archeology and Italian at the universities of Marburg, Bonn and Rome. She has lived in Florence for the past three years, where, as part of her doctoral work, she has been researching Ferraran painting of the 16th century. In addition, she leads travel study groups to various regions of Italy ("Shopping in Florence").

PHOTOGRAPHERS

Guidelines

INDEX